D1596758

The
Politician
Primeval

The Politician Primeval

From the Amoeba to the White House

EDGAR BERMAN

MACMILLAN PUBLISHING CO., INC.

NEW YORK

DISCLAIMER OF CREDITS

I wish to state unequivocally, without fear of contradiction, that I am not indebted, directly or indirectly, to my ever-loving and loved wife for aiding, abetting, or even encouraging this major opus.

Library of Congress Cataloging in Publication Data

Berman, Edgar.
    The politician primeval.

    1. United States—Politics and government—
1969-   I. Title.
JK289.B47   329'.00973   73-22527
ISBN 0-02-510060-2

Macmillan Publishing Co., Inc.
866 Third Avenue, New York, N.Y. 10022
Collier-Macmillan Canada Ltd.

FIRST PRINTING 1974

Printed in the United States of America

Contents

Preface

by Hubert H. Humphrey

Machiavelli advised his Prince what to do and how to do it. Edgar Berman shows all political "princes"—and political paupers—what they are and why they do what they do.

Machiavelli's counsel was empiric—he had not the benefit of either the facts of evolution or the modern sciences of anthropology, genetics, or ethology that Dr. Berman uses so well to explain the nature, character, and habits of the political animal. Up-dating the master is no mean feat.

Though Dr. Berman analyses the human politician in his inimitable witty, humorous, and ironical way, it should not mislead the reader into taking the underlying theme lightly. Before starting, I admonish the gentle readers interested in the most noble of pursuits—politics—to clear their minds of academic political cant and not reflexly object to theses that come from both a scientist and an astute political observer.

With rare good humor and wit, Dr. Berman mirrors the uniqueness and oddities and the foibles and limitations of politicians and voters alike, which they may not like but certainly can't deny. He holds them up to the cold light of their past and present and shows how it may well guide their actions in the future.

His thesis is certainly something to ponder by every politician

—and every constituent. Being a natural-born optimist (and maybe by the same token a politician), I do not totally agree with the finality of it all, but neither can I ignore its possibility.

I

Politicians Were Made in "Heaven"

(And in the Beginning—the Primeval Puddle)

I believe that if mankind proves for the fifth or sixth time that it is a hopeless political failure, then the same power that created us will create some sort of creature to carry on the work that has beaten us and thus make a political success.

—GEORGE BERNARD SHAW
The Political Madhouse in America and Nearer Home

Politics is the conduct of public affairs for private advantage . . . masquerading as a contest of principles.

—AMBROSE BIERCE
The Devil's Dictionary

Politics has always been considered a purely human failing. But observing Mr. Nixon in his natural habitat makes it perfectly clear that he and the profession he practices are neither pure nor entirely human. Though the politician may be loath to acknowledge his humble animal beginning, he wasn't born yesterday. The theories of Plato and Aristotle are only Johnny-come-latelies, and had as little to do with the beginning of politics as Freud or Masters and Johnson had to do with the mating game.

Before our ape ancestors became man—before they grew that extra layer of miraculous new cortical tissue onto their anthropoidal brains and were thus converted into god-fearing, respectable humans (soul and all)—they were political animals. Without the benefit of intellect each species had republics of

1

sorts, more the banana than the Platonic but still governments with chiefs, assistant secretary types and even vice presidents.

The Palpable Truth

Our modern political heritage goes way back in history. Politics began, not only before "intelligence" (which may be telling us something about politicians), but even before the primitive nervous system sprouted that bulbous knob of which it has since become so proud. Our earliest predecessor, the brainless microbe, found that he was not only more comfortable rubbing elbows with his brothers, but that he also lived longer by doing it. This awakening to the security of clustering, to the safety of the convivial life, was the prelude to politics. Without thinking about it, those that clustered survived and lived to pass along their genes, regenerating only their clustering kind. And from among that clustering kind emerged the greatest clusterer of them all—the politician, who has since also passed his special talents along. Those others—those myriads of single-celled beasties who preferred privacy and went it alone—died prematurely, never to reproduce their loner strain.

Old pros like Lyndon Johnson or Richard Nixon may bristle at the association of their sophisticated political reactions with those of a bacillus in the lower intestinal tract (the tiny microbes might be equally offended), but all politics can be traced to our earliest beginnings in the warmish green scum of a primeval puddle. Even then, those little animalcules knew in their protoplasmic "bones" what every South Boston ward heeler knows in his: Survival is sticking together. It was a portent of things to come—herds, schools, packs, and eventually Democrats and Republicans.

Just as those hordes of organisms were reassured by huddling and milling about (at that time, with no order and no organization), so are we all. Under a microscope, the frenzy of those one-celled little animals for closeness and security conjures up nothing so much as the body-to-body jostle of the Hudson County (New Jersey) faithful at their annual Democratic jamboree. On closer study, the difference between the two is academic.

The Touchables

All human political life, from the hippie communes at Big Sur and the garden clubs in Westchester to Congress and the United Nations, unknowingly has the selfsame agglomerating drive. On the stump or on the floor candidates and elected officials may attribute their tendency to touch the "peepul" to every motivation from religion and order to peace and love. In reality, it is no more ideologic, theologic, or intellectual than the bunching of a school of minnows.

Caucuses, quorums, committee luncheons, and indigestible banquets (or sit-ins and confrontations) are merely excuses for huddling and milling, mainly for those with just a little more than the average political tendency. No matter the droning dullness or chaotic excitement, they are happily "in touch." Like their insect forbears, their antennae are constantly searching to feel.

These pleasures of the politically driven reach ecstatic proportions in the climactic national conventions. The heat, the noise, and the inconvenience can't overcome the longing to feel and be felt. Causes and issues, planks and platforms, are half-forgotten (even by the New Left) in the exhilaration of the crowd. Lobby jams, traffic tie-ups, and queues for inedible food are not only patiently endured, but actually sought out. It's contact that counts. To palpate and be palpable is to be reassured that they have survived, and even more that they are loved—the everlasting goal of both the amoeba and the politician.

Even in this age of mass communication, where one television spot is worth a thousand baby kisses, some inordinate primordial urge to mingle and touch draws the political top drawer like George Wallace or Teddy Kennedy out of the TV studio and into the windblown airport rallies to "press the flesh" as LBJ put it. And though campaign managers may rail against this wasted motion, there is more to it than meets the eye. As with the Lord and Adam on the Sistine ceiling, there is some miraculous transferral of energy with the fleeting brush of the fingertips; the politician comes alive and the voter is reassured.

Libido and the Four-Year Itch

The strength of the political drive has never been equaled. To paraphrase Henry Kissinger (who should know): "Power is the greatest aphrodisiac." Sigmund Freud was wrong in his assertion that sex is the prime mover of men, for in the beginning, politics preceded sex. Those original bits of primitive life banded together for security way before carnal pleasure was even invented. Those genderless one-celled animals obviously enjoyed politics even before the ecstasy of splitting down the middle to reproduce was known, much less the pleasures of foreplay. Politics, not sex, began with life, and for the politician, it remains primal.

In a tropical ant hill or in the halls of Congress, the precedence of politics over sex still holds. Not one politician in a thousand—no matter his concupiscence—would trade his power for passion. Neither Richard Nixon nor Richard Daley would think of sacrificing his political lust for sexual lust (more's the pity). This failing is less a matter of romantic incapacity than the compulsion of an inborn priority.

The strength of the political versus the sexual drive can be compared in a simple aquarium experiment. When the water is warmed, a guppy's sex drive is lulled into a state of impotence. But it has little or no effect on his will to dominate the bowl and lead his school with an iron fin.

Though the established priority is undoubtedly political, this should not lead one to impugn the fabled libidinous proclivities of our human politicians. When power's abroad, can sex be far behind? History shows that where there is political smoke, there is sexual fire (though Presidents Harding, FDR, Kennedy, and LBJ's rumored trysts are omitted from the texts).

Political Darwinism

When one thinks of evolution, there usually comes to mind only the physical adaptation of animals to their surroundings. The chamelion is still around because in time of danger he

blended in with his environment, and the anteater thrived because he could stomach his peculiar diet. All life adapted
physically to survive. Eating ants was better than extinction.

In evolution or revolution it's also politics or perish. It's
only the "pol" who fights and runs away to live and fight
another day. Any species that has survived owes its success
as much to political as to physical adaptation. Was it not
the back-room shenanigans of the crafty baboon leaders (certainly not their muscle or that ridiculous furry coat in a steamy
jungle) that protected them from their feline enemies and
guaranteed their continuity? In the tiny termite it was obviously
its inborn political genius, not its size or strength, that allowed
it to proliferate and prosper.

As eating ants was better than physical extinction for the
anteater, eating crow is better than political extinction for the
politician. Richard Daley needed no Darwinian counsel on
crow eating nor political adaptation—not with a hamadryas
baboon on his family tree. When he saw Adlai Stevenson III's
handwriting on his Cook County wall, the powerful little
Chicago mayor adapted like a polar bear to an iceberg. A year
or so later, Adlai III also adapted by helping ease what he
had previously called that "corrupt Daley machine" back into
office.

On the other hand, our natural museums abound in skeletal
specimens of once-flourishing species of seemingly indestructible
physiques, all now extinct because they didn't know a good
deal when they saw one. The hulking dinosaurs probably didn't
have the sense to come in out of a glacier or to organize
against the saber-tooth. They had no more political savvy
than La Follette and his Populists, the Strom Thurmond
Dixiecrats, or the New Left "pointy heads" now all relegated
to the footnotes of political history.

Up the Organization

But politics is more than just clustering and adapting. There
is a natural ingredient dear to the politician's heart that makes
all the gears mesh: organization. Put any ward boss in a back

room with ten new precinct workers and there will emerge a proud captain, three willing lieutenants, and six block corporals with marching orders in hand and a plan to deliver on election day.

Though organization is now a labor of love, at one time it was organization or termination. Early on, it was a tossup whether life in all of its diversity would breed to the point of chaotic numbers and disappear—or organize. We're still here, so at one stage we obviously took the route of the bee and the termite and worked out a system (had we stopped at the bee or ant we might have been better off; the higher we've gone, the worse organized we've become).

Even that rotund South Side Irishman, Daley, needed aught but to tear a page from one of those invertebrate's political manuals to guarantee success to his beloved Cook County. This average Midwestern bailiwick controls Chicago, most of the state, and even influences the nation, but hardly by dint of its superintegrity, its morality, or its financial strength (politically disheveled New York can buy and sell Illinois).

Political Hives

In 1960, it was the organization of that well-disciplined Chicago apiary that took Illinois by 8,858 votes (out of nearly five million) and, according to the Republican rendition, burgled the White House for JFK. Even the Democrats admitted it wasn't intellect, it wasn't academic political science, it wasn't a grand strategy that turned the tide. It was that organized army of hustling runners, precinct captains, ladies' auxiliaries, and ward leaders with an abundant loyalty to a cause and a little larceny in their hearts that did the trick. They left no gravestone unturned in getting the ballots marked. Those busy devotees of the political art may get their take-home pay from the Bureau of Sanitation or the Department of Streets and Lights, but their real work is that of the Lord's and Dick Daley's in the vineyards of democracy.

They are a tight little island, loyal to a fault. They never miss a club night, hawk their quota of testimonial tickets, and deliver the Thanksgiving turkeys and Christmas toys. They diligently canvass their blocks and tend the polls like corpse watchers at a wake. When the word comes down from the Mount to "single shoot," "split the ticket," or "down the line," it fans out like a radar wave to every corner bar and newsstand and—it shall be done.

The Mostest and the Leastest

Aimless chaos wasn't transmogrified into organization overnight. In the tedium of evolution, a mutant gene different from all others suddenly appeared. It produced an anomaly that had a mania for organization, marble halls, and pomposity. The politician was born. Every strain of every species since has spawned this subspecies. In the crap shooting of genetics, by an absurd statistical probability (that no Las Vegas gambler in his right mind would take) there fell together a peculiar mix of chromosomes carrying traits such as sensitivity, arrogance, curiosity, appetite, perversity, extremism, cautiousness, and an abiding protoplasmic discomfort that couldn't stand disorder. It's sometimes called charisma.

The politician came about not by brawn, brains, or conditioning, but simply by birth, and has since passed his heritage along to generation after generation. Since arriving on the scene, the politician has led and organized. All those left over have followed. Without these two almost opposing components —leader and follower—evolution would have stopped with the *algae* and would never have produced queen and worker, gander and gaggle, politician and voter. However, this ridiculous alliance works only as all alliances work, when there is something in it for both of them. Both got and still get theirs—power for the few and security for the many.

Of the two, the ones that led were by far the stranger. Nature has produced some outlandish specimens, as witness the three-toed sloth and the armadillo, but in the politician she outdid herself. This mystical mutant whose genes are programmed to attract the faithful follower in flea or human must have come about for good reason. To have gone to such extremes, nature was obviously sending us a message. Only Darwin deciphered it. It was: "Onward, upward, or out." And so by that particular genetic offshoot, that dominant herring, that aggressive orangutan or our most ancient ancestor that egomaniacal australopithecine, the fish were led onto land, the ape down from the tree, and the Neanderthal to hallowed halls. Though this unique congeries of traits embodied in the politician is most difficult to live with, it was impossible to live without, and so our leaders have grown and prospered.

But no matter how leadership manifested itself by a thousand quirky combinations in a million different species, there was (and is) one common denominator. They all (somehow) attract a following. Exactly why the head aardvark or asp has loyal fans and fanatic followers is a mystery, but genetic attraction must play a large role. When the recently discovered *double helix* (those tiny strands in every cell in every organism which lead us by the nose) is finally unraveled, we will know why a plague of hungry locusts followed only that one locust honcho into the land of the Pharaohs; and why (other than the word from the Mount) the Israelites followed only Moses out. Whether or not we ever get to the bottom of it, it's the same genetic brand that leads a swarm or a Fourth of July parade.

So, from the start, with each begatting, there was propagated that identical strain—according to the laws laid down by that "mad" abbot, Mendel, a hundred years ago. This first geneticist, piddling away in his little garden, showed that by crossing certain colored sweet peas, he could predict the shades of colors of the offspring. Since then, in fruit flies, poodles, and man, he's been proved right. And so, each cell of every politician is programmed for his special knack just as the musician's or mathematician's is—by his genes. The ward leaders and precinct captains inherited a modicum of that genetic potential. Nixon, Mao, and Brezhnev are surfeited with it. And at whatever level he operates, the politician reflects the same characteristics inherited from that one ancient alpha gene, from that original leader bug, now memorialized in some ancient amber or in volcanic ash.

They Also Ran

Then there was that "other gene"—the leastest, the one in those who followed. Those follower traits are passed along also, no differently in the grub than in the genius. If he is at all politically inclined, he is just what the leader ordered—one of the organizables. He is a gullible, affable, acquiescent, dogged lemming right down to the water's edge. He is just right for the leader because the caliber of unfinished politician so far developed couldn't tolerate, much less lead, something more.

This follower-voter is programmed to achieve his one great goal—a long and safe, if tedious, life. Living by headlines, clichés, and ten-second spots, his particular genetic pattern makes Gallup predictions a cinch and Univac prophecies a sure thing within minutes after the polls close.

It may seem perplexing that the voter, the constituent, the subject, can be so different from his volatile, erratic leader when they both come from the same general seed. But then, how can the gentle, loving chimpanzee have ancestors in common with the nasty aggressive macaque monkey? It's all in what was needed to survive and how each was bent by his history. It is doubtful whether once bent, any could ever be unbent. No amount of conditioning, education, legislation, or PR can remake an instinctual creature that took well over a billion years to mature.

In the give (of the leader) and the take (of the ever-complaining follower), for better or for worse, the politically fittest and the great game of politics have tentatively survived.

II

Genetic Puppetry

(*Dancing to the Tune of the Gene*)

It is universally accepted that the characteristics of each particular person have their basis in the genetic endowment acquired at conception.

—René Dubos

Genes for various aptitudes exist in all social strata and professions—*including politics*. [italics added]

—Theodosius Dobzhansky

Yes, Virginia, there is a political gene. A twisted biological oddity compelling those whose ancestors had once led the pack and guided the gaggle to inspire men and lead nations. Even their campaign styles and pet bills and projects are more or less programmed at conception, like color blindness or cystic fibrosis.

Take a look at the flamboyant John Connally. Neither his gentle family life (a good Methodist upbringing) nor the intellectual(?) influence of the University of Texas could have conditioned him to take either to the pulpit or to the quiet statesmanship of Adlai Stevenson—no more than the instincts of the leopard could be gentled to those of a fawn. Nor could Julie Nixon (her father's daughter), had she been educated at Bennington, tutored by Marcuse, and had an affair with Jerry Rubin, be incited to burn her bra and picket for liberation. Political potential is as inborn and unchangeable as a zebra's stripes. Even a mediocre politician can't be fabricated from poor political genes.

Pavlov may have been able to make a poodle salivate

at the sound of a bell but he could never condition him to hunt a rabbit. Conditioning can neither make nor break a political drive. The worst of adversity couldn't have detoured the rampant political bent of that fighting cock HST and kept him in that Kansas City haberdashery nor buried that political mastodon LBJ in a classroom. *When you've got, you've got —when you've not, you've not.*

Fruit Flies Don't Lie

As Jane Goodall has observed in her jungle watch over the years, our tree-swinging ancestors dominate little differently from the mayor of Hoboken or a distinguished congressman from the Bronx, and they pass their dominance down to some of their offspring, depending on the genes of the particular political beauty they mate with. The carbon copies are produced exactly the way Monk Mendel predicted they would be from his sweet pea experiments a hundred years ago. Every high school biology student now knows that by crossing blue- and brown-eyed fruit flies (which breed a generation in a week), every combination can be bred and every possibility accurately foretold.

Those little fruit flies don't lie. And with the recent discovery of the key to life itself—the double helix (those fragile strands that program us like a computer)—we know more surely that the key to 1600 Pennsylvania Avenue lies in the fruit fly's case history. Since the genetic code is now broken, it is but a matter of time before we will be able to explain at birth why Shirley Chisholm acts differently than Marilyn Monroe, and why Ronald Reagan and George McGovern are not political birds of a feather. As the technique is refined, scientists will show that different genetic horsepower gives us block captains or presidents, just as it gives us lop ears or a balding scalp. They'll be able to spot who can and who can't spontaneously pontificate in any subject, throw out the first ball, kiss a thousand babies, and digest a rubber tire in the shape of a banquet chicken.

Martyrs Anonymous

But who among us will preach this un-American heresy in a society where every mother's son is a potential president and the alma mater guarantees a shot at it? Who will risk the fury of a female scorned as her hand is loosed from rocking the cradle that will rule the world (or argue with the proud daddy who, if not dandling a future president, is at least grooming an O. J. Simpson)? What modern-day martyrs will take the hounding that Galileo and Copernicus took when they came to the absurd conclusion that the earth was round?

No red-blooded American need knuckle under to this scientific truth—it can't happen here, the Constitution says so. If you're born equal, you can become anything you want and an AB degree proves it. At least that is what we've taken it to mean. The wail of the ADA, the Ripon Society, and the American Civil Liberties Union can already be heard in the land. "It's not nature, it's nurture and a U.S. citizen is no fruit fly."

The psychosocial behaviorists in the backwaters of science will likewise cry a lusty havoc, invoking the evils of the "Brave New World," Nazism, genetic engineering, and assorted varieties of nasty social sequelae. And our learned (untenured) pedagogues will jiggle their placards and chant Nurture, *si!* Nature, *no!*

"Sins" of the Father

But to no avail. The political apple, like all the less rotten ones, will not fall too far from the tree. The talent of the politician is handed down father-to-son (with the right mother mix) no less than that of the genius with the computerized mind or the brain born to compose sonatas. Senator Robert Taft, Jr. (the son) espouses the conservative causes of his illustrious father and grandfather (with identical grimaces and inflections), and the many facets of the liberal, twice presidential candidate Adlai Stevenson are indelibly stamped on the new Senator Stevenson of Illinois. And young "Humman" of the Georgia Talmadge clan metaphorically snaps his red galluses in debate, reminiscent of his red-clayed daddy in filibuster thirty years before.

The "Young Winston" is an even better example, inheriting not only political ideology but identical style from those tyrannical protoplasmic dots. The *Daily Mail* at the turn of the century noted that Churchill had his mother's political ways and talents and his father's ideology and habits.

> He is what he is by his breeding. From his father and his father's father he derived the hereditary aptitude for affairs (*not Jennie's kind*) [italics added] and the grand style of entering them. And from his American mother and her father a keenness, a shrewdness, half cynical; a personal ambition, a natural aptitude for advertisement and happily a sense of humor. Winston has not studied to be a demagogue—he was born one and happens to know it.

This could hardly have been the result of conditioning, for almost from his opening caterwaul he was in effect abandoned to the tender care of his beloved, if apolitical, nanny and then to boarding schools. He inherited his political talent, much as he inherited the slight lisp and the identical stance (hand on hip), from his father. It couldn't have been otherwise, for from the little affection he received from his father he could not have looked to him as an idol, a mentor, or even an example.

A Ring in the Nose

As much as all of us mortals are on the end of a tight genetic tether—the politician has not only a bull ring in his nose, but a prod at his rear. The inherited characteristics common to all politicians—ego, dominance, and aggressiveness—actually drive that unique creature (man or animal) to the most noble of callings, brooking no adversity and tolerating no obstructions. Basically, they are all alike; they differ only in inherited penchants and peccadilloes of style more recently acquired.

What better example of innate political compulsion, action,

and manner than JFK, a product of that prolific fount of the subspecies *Politicus americana*—the lace-curtain Irish? John could take or leave his love for law, literature, women, art, and the good life, all inherited honestly from Joe and Rose Kennedy. But he could no more opt out of politics than pronounce Cuber Cuba. He was at the beck and call of those ultramicroscopic dots passed down by old Joe and Joe's politician father, combined with those from one of Boston's great old pros, "Honey Fitz," his maternal grandfather, through Rose.

Those tiny particles in every cell of his body gave him the basic ingredients of his own fizzing formula of intellect, emotions, courage, and caution that guided him in every thought he had or action he took. His crucial decision in the Cuban missile crisis was decided not in the fall of 1962 in the White House, but some forty-five years before in *Rose's oval womb.*

This is not to say that when the Cuban crisis arose, psychologic lights blinked, mental bells rang, and robotlike he sent the U.S. fleet steaming into the Caribbean. But it does mean (give or take a little) that because of the "sins" of the father and grandfather (back *ad infinitum*) the character vested in him would react each time similarly in a similar situation. By his *dot-age* he could only respond to the Soviet challenge in his own special way, as he answered the steel strike with his midnight subpoenas and chose the stereotype of the "Best and the Brightest" to run his shop. He followed the guidelines of his original genetic wiring—for he could do nothing else.

Two to Tango

If those Mendelian track odds on the Kennedys and the Churchills were such sure things at such short prices (as has since proved itself in Bobby, Teddy, and probably Eunice if given half a chance), what happened to an odds-on favorite on the genetic tote board—the incomparable political genes of FDR? The scientific handicappers explain that if they can statistically predict the number of dominant blue-eyed flies when bred to brown-eyed females and the number of recessive brown-eyed duds that will come up, why not political duds? Clearly, it takes two to tango and FDR (related to eleven former presidents) drew a blank with Eleanor. Even if she had been as political as she seemed, the mix was not there. The proof of her political pudding was in her progeny. All four Roosevelt boys with all their conditioning, experience, and associations were "also-rans," minor short termers, or political flops. Today they collectively couldn't win a primary in their ancestral home, Hyde Park.

That Giant Puppeteer in the Sky

There's no getting around those little braided threads that jerk politicians this way and that and ultimately control us all. They surely nod the head, squint the eye, and ventriloquize the ayes and nays of the Charlie McCarthys on the floors of the legislatures, just as the similar but different invisible threads attached to the followers raise the arm that pulls the lever that marks the ballot that puts them there. But try to convince a politician (much less a social psychologist) that from the time that certain sperm impregnates that particular ovum, all are manipulated as if by a giant puppeteer high in the domes of power busily pulling the strings. Would that skeptical Missourian Harry Truman or that cynical Richard Nixon believe they are programmed and prepackaged from birth? Could their egos face the fact that neither their free will nor their superbrains but some strange force from a few invisible specks chose their party, cast their vote, and "fired the shot heard round the world"?

Harry might have been convinced if he had let Jane Goodall or Louis S. B. Leakey take him by the hand and show him himself swinging from branch to branch, jutting his jaw and barking his falsetto reminder that "the buck stops here." Or if Richard Nixon could be importuned to drop in at a laboratory he would make no mistake about his white mouse counterpart being reproduced scientifically, at this point in time.

They would then recognize a furry little Truman or a Nixon in a litter as easily as they could spot a table-hopping presidential candidate at a hundred-dollar-a-plate dinner. They could observe how mating those chosen ones (mainly male) with the right female (more difficult to spot) would in a few generations breed monkeyish Trumans or micey Nixons going about the business of protecting their interests, adjusting constituent complaints, and sitting in at summit conferences.

Neither would like it but they couldn't deny it. In defiance, they might question: "What does this have to do with humans?" As Louis Armstrong said about digging jazz or J. P. Morgan about the exorbitant upkeep of a yacht, "If you have to ask about it—forget it." Because if after over a hundred years of Darwin, Mendel, and Galton you still can't see the thick-skinned, resilient, resourceful traits of a baboon politician or a eugenically-bred mouse leader in a tough South Philadelphia cop who now runs our third largest city—"forget it."

The Sexist Sperm Plot

Again, the gene is the culprit if it is assumed (and it must be at least for now) that the male controls practically all of world politics. For only that wriggling little powerhouse, the male sperm, has the option of carrying either the male or the female chromosome (the deciding vote) as he is unmindfully shot into the hurly-burly of vaginal life. The lovely little ovum he is attracted to carries only the female one. So if he carries the XX sex chromosome, the progeny will be just another female, if it's the XY, it'll be a male—and thus a potential pol. Even here, blatant sexism rears its ugly head, as he and only he can decide—either bestowing that political taint—*for males only*—or not. He and only he can carry almost exclusively all of the unattractive traits necessary for political success (with due apologies to two of nature's genetic sports, Shirley Chisholm and Bella Abzug).

But could our major assumption be all cockeyed? It may be pure unliberated male brainwashing that has put males in control. It could be sheer coincidence that just a handful of the million or more animal species are led by females. For as the feminists insist the male cabal works in wondrous—and devious—ways. What would one expect when our two top politicians, Ted Kennedy and Richard Nixon, are ranked by

Ms. as number 1 and number 2 in suppressing female political aspirations (with another political type, Pope Paul VI, a close third).

Of Silk Purses and Sows Ears

If any of this shows anything, it's that the old "silk purse and sow's ear" theory is just as valid for politicians as for purses. But the "little genetic dictator" doesn't get a totally free ride. As the clay is molded, there are a thousand conditioning fingers ready to put their prints on it—and they do. The tougher the clay, the fewer the prints. Certainly JFK's glaze was imprinted and colored by his family's ambitions, his life in the London Embassy and at Harvard College. But even if he had come from South Boston and attended Dropsie University night school, the state legislature and the House of Representatives would never have held him.

The circumstances of a lifetime—a tough-minded mother, a rum-running father, a death in the family, or an impressive college professor—can blur the guidelines, but they will never erase them.

For instance, had sow-ears-like Ronald Reagan been reared in Lambaréné under Albert Schweitzer's *reverence for life* it would not have dented his basic irreverence for "welfare chiselers," or his lack of compassion for the jobless or disenfranchised. However, had he been conditioned by socialist Norman Thomas or Communist leader Gus Hall, he may have loosened a bit on less fundamental items, such as a small hike in the minimum wage law or allowing welfare mothers a few extra dollars for cost-of-living rise.

On the other hand, never in a thousand years could the most rigid, wealthy, conservative, and social family conditioning have controlled that mutant gene which made Averell Harriman reject his manor-born legacy. (The only obvious residuals from his early life were his courtly manner and his mellifluous broad *a*, which must have been a strange and foreign sound to the ears of Bronx-Gaelic Democrats or former ADA Chairman John Roche.) Harriman could no more have avoided the dictates of the political slots and grooves in his genetic punch card than willingly spend a weekend at Grossingers with rock singer Alice Cooper. It's real power when those miniscule dots in the chromosomes can pull off this bucking of the Establishment's Establishment, creating a sow's ear from old Ave's silk purse.

But with all their power, those little devils have never been accused of abusing it. They're even-handed, with not a snobbish strand in their earthy threads. Just as they guide the high and mighty, they divide the rank and file into Democrat, Republican, or Independent. The follower, the voter, the constituent, begets his political likeness no differently than his leader. Early imprinting or family pressures may instill some lifelong nasty habits and a few neuroticisms but will rarely reverse a voter's party penchant. Were a drab and doleful donkey (no Democratic analogy intended) suckled by a thoroughbred mare, it could never become a *Secretariat*.

The Dream Machine—Education

Yet the Walden II bunch (those died-in-the-wool behaviorists) still repeat the Skinnerism that man is born pure—a neuter, as Rousseau put it, a *tabula rasa* (a clean slate): "Give me the infant; I'll put him in a box, ring the Pavlovian chimes, and return him to you as per your order." How could they sell this, knowing that Pavlov's own *landsmen*, the Stalinists, rang all the political conditioning bells they could pull for over fifty years and yet few Muscovites, much less those fiercely independent Georgians, salivate over the Soviet political plums when they hear the chimes. Alas, the conditioning Skinner box even failed Skinner himself—for neither his daughter nor his grandson turned out exactly as prescribed.

Though the tenacious Soviets have now given up on Pavlov (via the great advocate, Lysenko) and the communes here have disappeared into thin air because the nature of man couldn't take such perfect order, belief in political conditioning is not stone cold in its grave. Who among us will ever give up on the great American Dream Machine—*Education!* Cherry pie and the thirty-year mortgage are no more American than the common man's equalizer, his great leveler, his great hope, the lullaby to the Harlem cradle, the folk song of the second-generation ethnic—and Portnoy's mother's entrée to the world of doctors' mothers.

And the Truth Shall Set Them

But the time has come. Just as the kiddies must be told at puberty about the birds and bees, so they should know *they'll vote just like their parents at age thirty.* Blood is thicker than Pepsi. A Mississippi redneck, a Philadelphia stiffneck, or a no-neck zealot of the New Politics already exists in the tiny blob of tissue nurtured in the womb. Even the counterculture Turks, exposed to all the pressures of the Far Left, hated themselves when the Gallup poll showed they voted exactly like their despised providers during the collegiate uprisings of the sixties, and again in 1972 when over 50 percent of them went for Mr. Nixon—that charred figure of a president, weekly burned in effigy on every college campus.

The clue to it all was obvious. The offspring in his hot dissent rejected any and all advice coming from parents. Why would they accept their political training if they wouldn't their toilet training? Pundits Harris and Scammon should have known from this alone that the vote is inherited like grandfather's watch.

Yet the syrup of conditioning is too soothing and hopeful to give it up so easily.

The research of that pioneer eugenicist Galton told it all about a hundred years ago. He showed then that twins, separated at birth and brought up in different households, weren't much different in their tastes in food, jobs, mates, hobbies, or hangups. Today studies of foster-home children reinforce this. It's even more the genes than the family problems that give us schizophrenics, alcoholics, manic depressives—and even homosexuals. So why not Democrats and Republicans?

Education may train a boy to be a dentist or social psychologist, but as the Harvard psychology professor emeritus Herrnstern has shown, it can't raise his I.Q. more than 15 percent, or change his emotional makeup, or make him more energetic or curious, or even slant his reaction to a color or a sex object. So how could it have converted a Rennie Davis first into an SDS radical, then into a spokesman for a fifteen-year-old guru. Could Harvard have opened Joe Namath's pass-tossing synapses to the theory of relativity? No more than Einstein's reflexes could be trained for a fade-out fake reverse.

As the Gene Goes—So Goes the Politician

Education or no, nature or nurture and John Lindsay notwithstanding, it's a rare mayor, governor, or congressman who is not in the party to which he was born. Example doesn't change the basic tot and education doesn't change the basic politician. Hubert Humphrey's graduate education at conservative Lousiana U. didn't swerve him from his civil rights gambit at the 1948 Democratic Convention any more than a Reed College doctorate would have changed Senator Roman Hruska's support for Carswell and Haynsworth to the Supreme Court. On the other hand, if political potential could have been thwarted by poor education, LBJ would never have left the Pedernales nor Huey Long the bayous of Cajun country.

No matter the family life, peers, education, or outside influence, a particular political nature will soon be as predictable as the color of Mendel's sweet pea. With the secrets of the genetic code exposed more each day, it follows that political leanings will soon be diagnosed by the computerized science of genetic analysis.

One cell from a six-week-old fetus in the womb will not only tell us its sex-to-be and whether it will have sickle-cell anemia, it will also diagnose Republicanosis or even the degree of Democratitis. Each and every physical, mental, and metabolic characteristic of the voter will be coded and as easily read as an electrocardiogram. When perfected, this new science may even be able to detect the qualities of a political candidate. Who can tell what genetic deviations will label a politician? It may be in the nature of an extra Y chromosome, as in some sex criminals (then watch out for castrating Billy Grahams), or just the absence of a chromosome, as in a mongoloid idiot. (Now with sperm banks, we could even store the *semenly* perfect political seed of Senator Hugh Scott,

Richard Daley, or LBJ and with the proper matching ovum come up with Super-pro; and may the Lord have mercy on our souls.)

The breaking of the genetic code and the increasing use of Mendelian science in diagnoses of disease will create a new breed of political pundit, equipped with only a needle and computer. They will look upon our present political science as our present-day pundits now regard those ancient scanners of bird entrails for omens.

In its senescence, politics is coming of age. It may become the science of the probable rather than remain the beloved (if chaotic) art of the possible.

III

Politician Know Thyself

("*Mirror, Mirror . . . ?*")

Nine out of ten politicians are knaves who maintain themselves by preying on the idiotic vanities and pathetic hopes of half wits.

—H. L. Mencken

So what hath God wrought? What's become of that run-of-the-mill little leader gene now after the ups and downs of that long climb from that one-celled animalcule in the alluvial seas, onto land, into the trees, through college (and possibly graduate school), and now safely ensconced in hallowed halls. How much has that strange gene changed, reacting and adapting since it sprouted that remarkable new gray matter in its skull. How does it live now in the ecologic balance of the back rooms, the State house, and the husting; among the voters, the hangers-on, the lobbyists, and the do-gooders.

The human politician is basically still what he is, but somewhat different from what he thinks he is. Because of his privileged, if misspent, youth, of some millions of years based on the self-assumption that he was "heaven sent," he doggedly believes that the world owes him a living—like any other deity.

There is no doubt about how he sees himself even if there is great doubt about how he is seen by others. No one respects and admires the politician as the embodiment of honor, justice, duty, sacrifice, and righteousness—more than he himself. His self-beatification naturally follows his firm belief that he was especially chosen to lead by his Maker, and his feeling of close kinship to that one and only divine offspring. Living with him is difficult at best because he has fewer doubts about his innate endowments than Paul of Tarsus had on the road to Damascus (he was born—Paul was made). If, as he expects, stigmata do appear, there may be even greater problems

Saint or Sinner

One can sum up his essence in simple terms—*hubris, chutzpa, gall*—political virtues he has earned the hard way. These dubious chevrons were gained on the pitted battlefield of evolution by means that would hardly qualify him as a candidate on the sainthood ticket. He led all of us up the evolutionary ladder step by step, the hard way, unhampered by character or convictions. On almost all counts he (and we) should have disappeared as a species; instead he's brought us up from the murky reaches of the beginning. Understandably he is unnourished by the milk of *human kindness* nor does he yet live by lacey-gloved garden-club standards. If he had been, his most potent globular parts would have long since been pressed like desiccated rose petals between the truth of the leaves of Machiavelli's great tome—and then where would we be?

Aristotle, one of the ancient innovators and critics of the noble art, had some prescience of political evolvement, for he labeled man a "political animal" twenty centuries before present-day ethologists proved it. However, he failed to point out that even as our leaders cloak themselves in lamb's fleece, they are more wolf than most of us. The politician was forced into the hustle from the day his safe arboreal paradise was rendered treeless and leafless by cataclysms of heat and glaciers. He led his chattering, curley-tailed troop down from the withered branches to compete with the big boys—the saber-tooth and the timber wolf, who were stronger, faster, and more lethal. He knew full well their taste and appetite for the tender fillets of the primate—namely, himself.

He did it and flourished—not only by his muscle, but also by his new wits and political know-how. There were all grades of him, just like his political-animal ancestors—the highest, alphas; the lieutenants, betas—all the way down to the near omega corporals.

The Old-New Politics

One-to-one the leader would have been a *goner*. He had to be more political than most to survive, for there was safety only in outsmarting his rivals. So he instinctively plagiarized (and embellished with lethal variations) a real New Politics directly from the shrewdest and most calculating of his forbears, the monarchial baboon. The tactics of that tough, mean, avaricious old uncle in his use of power and organization were passed down naturally. (Unlike other apes, who are fast disappearing, the baboon is prospering and even dying a civilized death of coronary heart disease—just like his pupil.) So our fragile new politician, using his innate teaming skills for hunting and defending, was soon able to organize his troops to kill and eat with the best of them rather than be killed and eaten like the worst (who vanished). He did it by hook and crook, deals and compromises, tooth and claw—little differently than he does it today.

There he now stands—barely biped, less hairy but fashionably less naked, hardly removed from the rain forest, but pretending he was never there as he tried to prove in the Scopes trial in Tennessee. If there is a modicum of self-delusion in him, there's just cause. How else could he look himself squarely in the eye and not see, peering back through the foliage, the glow of orbs partly baboon, partly leopard, and partly crocodile, and feel godly still? He feels a natural unease knowing a predatory beast lurks deep in his soul. Thank heavens that we, his constituents, have a taint of the same and show tolerance as he poses, threatens, intimidates, growls a warning or whines obeisance; demanding respect from the weak and giving respect to the strong; hiding his shortcomings and exhibiting his strengths, just like his political counterpart in a wolf pack. But as laureate Nikolass Tinbergen showed, man is a bit more "the only species that is a mass murderer." And who, but the friendly affable neighborhood politician has lead this on-going ritual since the caveman. He is hardly the generous Red Ridinghood he fancies himself.

The Gregarious Loner

To take the politician at face value is to take the biggest pig in the biggest poke. For instance, next to certain insects and bacteria the politician is the most gregarious beast invented, yet he is more a loner than the most reclusive leopard. His circle of friends is usually a plethora of one—if that. Even then, as LBJ found out, friends are risky business to a politician. Bobby Baker did him about as much good as John Mitchell did Nixon or Voloshen did Speaker McCormack.

The politician is only comfortable and secure in his own ego-massage parlor—a cheering mob of strangers or an applauding group of admirers, knowing there's political safety in numbers. But face to face, one to one, he becomes a loner leopard again, muscles tensed, tail slowly twitching, eyes searching, suspicious. A political survival mechanism, a means of conserving his power —his life—makes him leery of relatives, wary of colleagues, and scared to death of vice presidents. (JFK wouldn't dare turn his back to LBJ, nor LBJ to HHH, nor FDR to all three of his veeps—and the combination of the White House political vault was always in unbreakable code.)

The politician is always the poor little rich guy, worrying whether he's really loved for himself. No wonder (Fala) man's best friend was always close on the heels of FDR or that Lincoln would head for the understanding of the kennel after each bout with Mary Todd. When Hans and Fritz departed Nixon's company only King Timahoe's buzzer rang more than General Haig's.

The presidency, as often described, is the loneliest job on earth. But it's not the job, it's the man. The picture of a lone, preoccupied JFK, shoulders hunched, staring out of the Oval Office window onto the south lawn, is not one of the convivial politician—it was he as he was. And Nixon, as estranged from nature as a Skinner box baby, was often photographed head down, scuffling along a lonely beach, ruining his seventy-dollar hand-made Italian shoes, even before his Watergate headaches.

Though our hearts may go out to this pitiable figure of a man, he's less to be pitied than censored. Walter Lippmann must have been in one of his mellower moments when he said, "Politicians don't mean badly, most of the time they don't mean anything." The outspoken Congressman, Emanuel Celler (D., N.Y.), when recently (involuntarily) stepping down from his seat after fifty years of continuous service, galled his "esteemed" colleagues when he divulged the secret of their success. To paraphrase, he intimated that it is more important to have the persistence of a bill collector, the stubbornness of an ass, the intelligence of a moron, and the diplomacy of a way-ward husband than a learned doctorate in political science.

Idiots Delight—Sine qua Omnia

More than one reluctant political novitiate has been reassured before wetting his feet that intelligence is not a serious handicap to political fortune. As Henry Kissinger once said, "Intelligence is not all that important in the exercise of power and is often, in point of fact, useless. The leader neither needs nor uses intelligence."

Henry is right, yet for obvious reasons intellect is a trait wish-fully willed unto politicians by hopeful voters. Politicians them-selves view it as a mixed blessing—enjoying the sound of its being attributed to them, but knowing it is rarely a part of them. LBJ was in awe of, yet uncomfortable with, "that brilliant S.O.B. with the slicked-down Sta-comb hair, Robert McNamara, the former whiz kid and secretary of defense. Harry Truman had a special distrust of the political intelligentsia, accusing them of "paternalistic elitism," and the philosopher Santayana at Harvard knowing his own breed well said, "An academician in politics is a disaster."

These opinions may be on the extreme side, though there is little doubt that the twists and turns of political life demand less Aristotelian logic and psychologic theory than innate shrewd-ness and precinct experience. In the politics of the sixties, the ice-cold superbrains of the Bundys and Rostows bowed defer-entially (even when they differed) to the least intellectual (by his own admission) of Texas-type politicians.

However, we are beating a dead donkey (or elephant, as the case may be), for most political leaders past and present have never laid claim to abstract thought nor used the theoretical fundamentals of political science to gain their ends. In the act of governing, some of the most famous products of *Precinct U.*— Mayors Daley, Jimmy Walker, and Sam Yorty; Governors Huey Long, George Wallace, and Senator Herman Talmadge; Presidents Grant, Harding, and Eisenhower—had as little use (if less cognizance) of the philosophy of politics as Ivan the Terrible. Truth was in the winning.

Even in the legislative field, the names of the intellectually endowed are not too numerous. To take their measure one need go no further than a glance at the statute books—local, state, or federal, on everything from pornography to Prohibition —to understand what manner of mentality imposes its whimsy on its willing wards.

Other unessentials for political success are humility and integrity, for who with these human traits could offer themselves as presidential candidates seriously, in the full knowledge of the price they must pay?

Though the lesser virtues may be lacking, the sense of papal infallibility is a *sine qua non.* It obviously envelopes the politician more and more as he ascends into the political heavens, and at the peak, a little worship is expected. In the lower reaches, politicians temporarily settle for recognition, knowing full well that their deification is only a matter of time and landslide victories or abysmal defeats only hurry or delay it.

Blood of My Blood

Part of what every politician is must also be chalked up to his constituents. As Darwin showed, every species (and subspecies, including politicians) survived only because of its special endowments. If the politician's brain (Democrat or Republican) developed with the more monstrous instincts of the wolf or the crocodile rather than those of the lovable panda or the quick-witted dolphin, it did so because it is part and parcel of the particular constituency that spawned it. As the saying goes, they must deserve each other. If a bizarre politician is supported, it is a bizarre electorate that chose him. A hive of bees rarely trails even the most charming rhinoceros into the river, nor do polar bears leave their icy tundras to follow the most charismatic zebra into the jungle.

But within the breed, charisma (whatever that is) does count. It may be drawing too fine a line to impute even the most esoteric attraction to the bloodless President Coolidge or the plethoric Herbert Hoover (overflowing his celluloid collar), yet they must have evoked some kind of chemical reaction or subconscious empathy. The new science of population genetics shows that even the most insignificant of peculiar gene pools—albino, pygmy, Ku Klux Klan, or Dixiecrat—is guaranteed a leader, at the very least a Coolidge or Hoover, ready and willing (and sometimes able) to lead in a particular political condition, climate, or era. It explains why the flinty hard Montanans foster Mike Mansfield (the atrophied Senate majority leader) and the political pool of Los Angeles opted for the flamboyant, eratic Sam Yorty for three terms. It is just these genetic variables that make political as well as biological evolution work as well as it does.

A Sixth Sense or No Sense

It seems a toss-up whether politics takes more of a sixth sense or no sense at all. But it's his sixth sense, plus a few bizarre instincts and habits harking back to his *Homo habilis* boyhood, that makes a politician lead, not follow.

In the day-in-day-out give-and-take of politics, it's the sixth sense—an instinct (not the new intellect, which frequently gets in the way)—that separates the man from the boy politician. Political decisions, as Hubert Humphrey said, are made by "the feel of the hair on the back of your hand." It's either political intuition or political malnutrition.

Politicians live to regret leaving political decisions to experts, academics, or even former account executives. As JFK sadly learned from the Bay of Pigs, a pro takes all the advice he can get—but trusts only his viscera. (Who knows? There may be something to reading political entrails.) On the hustings his closest brain trusters and administrative assistants, so brilliant in matters substantive, have proved themselves deadly in matters elective. Intuitively bankrupt, they couldn't win a fixed PTA primary in South Jersey. Ken O'Donnell, Arthur Goldberg, Pierre Salinger, Sarge Shriver, Ted Sorensen, and lesser ones too numerous to mention have all run for everything from caucus delegate to governor to U.S. senator to vice president—or anything up for grabs—some two or three times. No wins.

For the political gene will out. There are no ersatz politicians and sooner or later the real politician stands up. Those straight-laced genes can't be fooled for very long (though sometimes too long), and though lightning may strike, it's rarely twice in the same place.

Former Senator Joseph Tydings of Maryland found that looks, money, friends, marriage partner, and a distinguished name (which was thankfully changed from Cheeseborough to the more politically influential one of his stepfather Senator Millard Tydings) weren't enough. He had everything going for him but the sixth-sense gene. As hard as he tried, he was stiff in a crowd of partisans and frozen in the warmth of a tavern. Precinct workers sensed his *noblesse oblige* and his blue eyes watered in a smoke-filled room. He lost after one term to a nonentity (Glenn Beall), but a nonentity with gene appeal gotten from his father, a senator before him. His younger brother, George Beall, seems to have even more—he is the U.S. attorney in Maryland who pulled the props out from under one of the great political mistakes of all times—Spiro Agnew.

Agnew was a lightning phenomenon, striking thrice in the same place—a fluke upon fluke. Though he went far beyond himself, genetic justice finally put him out to pasture and almost in jail. This less-than-mediocre political talent was strained to its political limit at the PTA level, but curiouser and curiouser, he rose first to be an undistinguished suburban county executive, then to become a pus-poor governor of Maryland, and finally he arrived as the abysmal Nixon running mate in 1968. Each time lightning struck he was deemed the lesser of two evils (a title he can no longer claim), as he stumbled higher and higher all the way to the political bank—then political bankruptcy.

In the animal world, the follower once fooled turns off, rebels, or just becomes neurotic and doesn't reproduce—leaving the leader high and dry. There is no need for postmortems, but secure in the knowledge of mammalian genetics and politics, we may say that Mr. Agnew was due for extinction as surely as his pterodactyl ancestors were—it was only a matter of time.

Labor Pains and a Day of Wrest

Observing the political mentality for one day in a campaign explains more than would a three-year probe on the couch. What psychiatrist could analyze the insanities (much less the inanities) of the politician's daily life? How does the politician even explain to himself (without acute embarrassment) slogging out to a plant gate in a subzero Wisconsin dawn to give a fleeting, if benumbed, smile and a frozen handshake to thousands of blurred faces hurrying in for their morning coffee? Then continuing on with daredevil helicopter stops in a blizzard—first to deliver a major fiscal policy address to a dozen or so of the more hardy of a ladies' auxiliary who've braved the elements, then on to an in-depth explanation of the SALT talks to a Kiwanis booster club of local dairy farmers at the high school gymnasium fifty miles away. After a much-needed 4 P.M. luncheon break of Spam and beans, it's back to the city for the mayor's pet skid row project—a soup kitchen—and the fourteen-hour day is polished off by getting into black tie for a church-catered "box dinner" at a Sheboygan Union Hall.

But politics is not just motion, charisma, and hangups. There is work—of a sort—in the process. Though it's a peculiar type of work neither manual or mental a politician straining to dislodge the one above or shake off the clutchings from below is no featherbedder. Unlike the profligate grasshopper who chirped all summer and starved in winter, the politician is like the assiduous ant with a summer-winter work hookup. Since his only happiness is in staying on top, his only job insurance is working at it. No sweatshop menial could match him. Even good union bosses like George Meany and I. W. Abel complain that they can't lead their workers to a utopian four-day week when political leaders set such a bad example.

Every good politician claims a close kinship with labor, but the life he leads proves otherwise. His habits would swell the heart of the NAM (if not an efficiency expert), as they would chill that of a shop steward. What shop steward worth his salt would feel better on the bench than on the beach or in a committee room than in a barroom? Where in the ranks of labor is retirement a dirty word? What ditch digger would brave the hazards to life and limb, from small plane crashes or assassinations, without the benefits of workmen's compensation?

Even the revered Sabbath is a day of *wrest* for the politician—without time and a half. However, he doesn't totally disregard the idea of a divine "four day weekend" (every political body in the land considers Fridays and Mondays sacrosanct *legislative* holy days). Sick leave? Paid vacations? No such thing. Even at Christmas and Easter, a politician wouldn't be caught dead anywhere but on a junket.

All Seven Deadly Sins

This may sound like a tedious life, but within the club, below the surface and mostly behind closed doors and at odd hours, political Jack is not a dull boy. Aside from the more gross iniquities of campaigns and conventions, there are more pleasurable emoluments and side benefits in politics, by accident, than there are on purpose in other professions.

Like a macaque monkey leader, elected officials soon get used to being groomed and serviced in style. If it isn't by volunteers or constituents, it's by administrative assistants, committee employees, and even the lint-brushing and door-opening Washington breed of parasites—the sociotodes like the Logans, the Cafritz's, and the True Davis'.

To get into the more lively fringe benefits, the decadent pleasures of the flesh cannot be discounted. These come as naturally to those elected as the choice cuts of game dragged in by the spouse to the lion chief, or the first crack at the female in heat to the species leader (whoever he is). All men are born decadent, but politicians are born more decadent than most. And contrary to popular belief, it seems not to affect their health or longevity—as witness John Adams parting the hustings at ninety, Madison at eighty-five, Jefferson at eighty-three, and Truman, Jackson, Van Buren et al. at ripe old ages.

Certainly the fleshpots of our Capital City are not designed for the enfranchised voter backbone of the Republic. Famous political watering places like the Sans Souci cater neither to administrative assistances, lesser cabinet officials, nor the tourist from Dubuque. Admission there is neither by the size of the holdings nor by the branchings of the family tree. The only entré and the only credit card accepted is *political*. It's ultra-fashionable "lunch counter" is anything but integrated for non-politicians. If you're not in maitre d' Paul's inner circle of White House or Congressional stars, it's back to McDonalds. No political sit-in could break this discrimination.

Kissinger's Complaint

There is no question that at the end of the political workaday, the sap seems to rise at the first taste of the traditional juice of juniper (with a touch of vermouth).

Though fun and food are the more well known extracurrcular niceties accorded political success, there are other official amenities. For the politician does not live by soufflés alone. Neither the grooming of the political ego, the sating of the political palate, nor the cool of the political mind can mollify the heat of the political loin. In fact, it is just the opposite. Though the work ethic pervades the world of politics, power does stimulate the smouldering libido, just as Mr. Kissinger admitted. (J. Edgar Hoover's dossiers on this little foible kept him on top—and politicians on edge—for half a century.)

Though this venal sin is taken for granted among the elected, the Washington press, unlike their more sensation-minded London colleagues, has been very good about keeping it under wraps. Though an alcoholic first lady or a homosexual in the White House is rarely headlined, *Parade* magazine did break the code by naming the four outstanding philanderers in politics—but they could have named a hundred and four with no surprises for the cognoscenti.

The private hideaway rooms in the Capitol for the solitude (to be sure) of uninterrupted thought and decision may also be used for the more relaxed conjugal "affairs" of state. (According to Bill Moyers, these nests are so hidden in the bowels of that grand edifice that one paramour of a prestigious senator waiting for her long-overdue statesman to return from a quorum call wouldn't dare venture out for fear of never negotiating the seemingly planned maze that led her there.)

The chauffered limousines are not only a luxury but also a handsome symbol of power; the prized offices with a view of the Capitol (suitable for framing with the principal gazing pensively out) are for those with seniority. Then, of course, there are the choice committees with salaried bodies expected to do routine chores from picking up the dry cleaning to getting the snow tires changed. As an added fillip, in the fall the politician is wined, dined, and regularly ticketed to the Redskins gratis, in a style befitting his status, as he travels in the jet-propelled circles of the famous and the extravagant.

John (the Baptist) Couldn't—Can Billy (Graham)?

So this is the politician as he is from the animal that he was. Naked as a jaybird, as Lippmann said, he doesn't seem half-bad, but as we all know, the fruits of his striving have been less than satisfactory. No one seems content with him but he himself, yet he hasn't been studied enough to see if he could be better.

The problem at hand in our just and Christian society, operating under egalitarian democratic principles, is how one tempers, if possible, a million years of those not-quite-humane, but nevertheless effective, political practices generated in the politician's bloodstream. The first step to improvement is to learn how he got the way he is. And the second is to determine whether if we tamper with his constitution we could make it worse. Reformers from John the Baptist to Billy Graham (with his prayer breakfasts regularly attended by our godly president, his pious staff, and those "nearer my God to thee" leaders of Congress) have tried. It may take more a cleansing of the chromosomes than of the soul, but we can't tell until we take a good look.

IV

The Body Politics

(*What Are Little Voters Made of?*)

> There is no public enthusiast alive of twenty years practical experience who believes in the political adequacy of the electorate—or the body it elects.
> —G. B. SHAW

> The Democratic man lives from day-to-day indulging the passions of the hour.
>
> —PLATO

The politician can never be understood without comprehending his most incomprehensible counterpoint—his follower, the foundation of the political system. But yet, the very theory of democracy, one of mankind's proudest achievements, has only one major flaw—this foundation. If Thomas Jefferson had only spent more time working this out instead of wasting his time on the plumbing at Monticello, we would all have been better off. It is indeed an idealistic, if presumptuous, proposition to rest *"the last best hope of man"* on the character and intelligence of its least (but very) common denominator—the voter. It is as if the architects of the Empire State Building decided to pile the millions of tons of steel and mortar on footings of putty. To risk the future of the species on the voter, whose creed is "better led than dead," was not exactly to give the system a running start.

A Follower is a Voter is a Follower

The enshrined voter, the enlightened, faithful, hopeful, charitable, civic-minded citizen with a free will, is known to exist—but difficult to unearth. This should be expected. Why should the human be any more unusual than the elephant follower? Enshrined or not, the follower still obediently follows like his pachyderm cousin single file, trunk to tail, as close to his bull as possible. And herein lies the problem. The human species has come a long way from its trunk-swinging, tail-switching ancestors, but its following instinct hasn't changed a whit. Thomas Jefferson et al. either didn't know or forgot this little item in their grand plan (which may cost them, and possibly us, a permanent place in history).

A follower is a follower is a follower, behind a lead goose, an alpha moose, or high man on the Congressional Roost. Whether serf, subject, or enfranchised voter, it's all the same. For he follows, not to keep up with the Joneses, but with his long-lost australopithecine ancestors. Since those early days, man has tried every scheme he could come up with; only following gave him what he wanted—a long, safe, tedious life. The priorities of eating regularly and avoiding a premature and violent end are not without merit, and he found these ends were more attainable just the way he's always gained them.

Nothing has changed this instinct: the Declaration of Independence didn't budge it, nor the Sermon on the Mount dent it, nor did "love thy neighbor" substitute for it. Even the power to vote didn't make it *inoperative*. It has stood man in good stead through glaciers, floods, and other natural cataclysms for a hundred million years, and he'd have been crazy to trade it for a beautiful, if shaky, experiment (at his expense) by an idealist like Thomas Jefferson, who was himself always broke and had to sell his library to buy a decent burial, or Robert Morris, a Declaration signer who wound up in debtors' prison.

A Grim Fairy Tale

We are all more or less dreamers and at one time or another believed in Cinderella, Mother Goose, and Shangri-la. But to seriously put the affairs of state—war and peace, poverty and prosperity—into the hands of those "deriving their just rights from the consent of the governed" is beyond fantasy, it's well into psychopathology. The National Institute of Mental Health estimates as many as six million red-blooded Americans with schizophrenic symptoms, nine million alcoholics, and many millions with anti-social behavior—all loose and able to vote. Sure, the voters can't be all bad, but allowing them to choose their leaders is like allowing the denizens of a nursery school to choose their teachers—which would unanimously be Chuckles the Clown. A flock of geese would never get farther south than Saskatchewan if it had to agree on who would lead the V-shaped formations to Miami.

"Government of the people, by the people, and for the people" would have perished from this earth if it had lived by its rhetoric. Luckily, these inspiring words are salted away, only to be hauled out for inspiration on the Fourth of July. Though these sparkling phrases don't interfere too much with government, an occasional busybody like Ralph Nader or John Gardner, with no pragmatic sense or perspective, tries to make the system live up to its oratory—which stirs up a lot of trouble.

But even if the voter aspires to be what he is touted to be (and he occasionally shows aspiring signs), he just isn't built that way. He can repeat after me until the coming of that long-postponed millennium, "I'm different, I have been endowed with a brain, a sacred franchise, and a choice, and will act like an independent human being," but he'll still hold tight to that tell-tail in front of him, following each giant step—even over the cliff—brain, franchise, and all.

The Proof in the "Pudding"

The voter's problem is that two hundred years of democracy have conned him into thinking otherwise. He is entranced with the idea of being human (and who wouldn't be?), but he's frustrated because it's a tough idea to live up to. It's not that he hasn't pathetically tried to act out the part assigned him—to study candidates and issues, make an intelligent choice, and cast a ballot for a better world—but it takes more than he's got. Little doubt, the brain was a marvelous gift, but one had to learn to use it—and most haven't (at least not the followers). And if after tens of thousands of years even the most sinewy muscles atrophy from disuse, what can be expected from the pudding-like cerebral hemispheres? The brain could have been created as smooth as a billiard ball for all the use made of its convolutions.

The little man in the voting booth is no doubt a well-meaning fellow. But that old instinct keeps nagging: "What about me? Who's minding the store while I'm identifying issues, weighing evidence, and deliberating?" Sure, in the long run that franchise is important, but more important is the short run. A hungry chimpanzee will choose a bunch of ripe bananas over a ten-carat diamond every time.

Participatory democracy, that great concession to the common man, is still held tightly to the voter's breast, with a concern and reverence ranking second only to the "God Bless America" on his woven sampler. But will it buy him a cup of instant security coffee? What's it worth on the shelf? Unlike those courageous signators of the Declaration who inspire him, the voter may voluntarily risk his sacred honor but never his life or his fortune.

The Fast Vote Franchise

So the common man's greatest blessing, the franchise to vote, fragile in the hands of philosophers, has not been as revered as Ben Franklin (specs and all) had expected. If Franklin had had the use of a giant cosmic telescope, he could not have glimpsed "what God hath wrought" on that humane idea. As earthy a philosopher as he, could not have envisoned trading this saving grace of the individual for a pint of Ripple in Harlem or a half-jug of "white lightning" in Appalachia on election day. He could not have been more surprised to see real lightning transmitted from a kite to a key than to see a vote being haggled for by "walking-around money" in Newark or South Philadelphia, or lobbyists (of every ethnic, business, labor, and church bloc) doing their wholesale bartering on the Senate floor as if on the floor of the Stock Exchange.

It's not easy for the voter to be what he is yet act what he isn't. That firm foundation of democracy is little different in his priorities than in those of a mother armadillo with four mouths to feed, but you'd never know it to hear him talk. The voter acts the part like an itinerant preacher. With eyes lifted to the heavens, he solemnly plays out his expected role as dedicated voter by speaking out, attending, helping, and organizing—a model major citizen. But at the moment of truth, at the lever-pushing ceremony, he does what he has to do as if he were Willie Sutton set free in Fort Knox.

Though the fairly uncomplicated garden variety of human does what he must, still he is torn, for though he is just a simple follower, he's been invested with vote power whether he can use it or not. He has become as schizoid as a two-headed calf.

Part of his problem is his congenital afflictions. He has a few inborn genetic aberrations such as gun-barrel vision that zeros in on security only, and an ear stone-deaf to political ethics. But his most serious pathology is a political allergy so clogging to the nasal passages that it makes the effluvia of demogogic garbage indistinguishable from the sickly-sweet aroma of a righteous funeral bouquet.

Passion Players

Actually, it's not fair to lump all voters into one common ball of genes. They may be brothers under the skull, with more passion than probity, but among them there are shades of difference. However they could only be detected scientifically by a genetic sampling of the blood or an electroencephalographic tracing—but they are there. Some broad categories are more obvious. Other than minors, felons, aliens, and the insane (and where is that line drawn?), who are not allowed to vote, the largest category of eligible voters are the votophobics. Come hell or the high dungeon of the League of Women Voters, they dig their heels in all the way—but only up to the polls.

They were importuned, exhorted, and embarrassed in the 1972 presidential contest, but (not unlike all other elections) about 40 percent of the eligibles stayed home in the general election and almost 90 percent went fishing in the New York primary. And just last year, 95 percent stayed in bed rather than cast their ballot for better education for the kiddies of our nation's capital. They avoid the voting booth as if they were claustrobes invited for dinner on a submarine.

Politophobes were force-fed by the media like a Toulouse goose, but these pâté-livered nonbelievers evaded the polls like that bird avoids the butcher's block. No one seems to understand; these nonvoters are not just lazy or turned off, they are just GNVs—genetic nonvoters. They have a recessive (if selective) political gene resulting in a heretical political personality that is resistant to all blandishments of democratic uplifting. They tolerate the Oral Robertses of the political circuit with their threats of fire and brimstone or promises of a voter's pearly gates as they thunder that there is no such thing as a bad voter. These political do-gooders, these registration drivers, try to make honest hymn-singing voters out of political skid rowers. But true GNVs (that solid 40 percent) are about as redeemable as the Happy Hooker.

Then there are those who do vote—Middle America, from plumber to professor. With them, it's a habit like going to church; they may not know why, but if they didn't do it, they'd feel guilty. This backbone of the democratic political system get their enlightenment principally from headlines, thirty-second spots, and the 7 P.M. news. They may not know anything about politics, but they know whom they don't like. And as long as they have their last-minute political crib—the sample ballot—in hand, they have a sense of confidence to bolster their ignorance. In their solitude behind the curtains, they studiously give the ample two to three seconds per candidate (or issue) and make each big decision. If a familiar name strikes a chord, they press the lever with decisiveness and conviction. An unknown shop foreman from South Boston named John F. Kennedy was twice elected as treasurer of Massachusetts by just putting his name on the ballot. If not, the franchise may be consummated by the suffix ("ski," "stein," "dale," or "ez") closest to their hearts. And all things being equal they will press Abel's lever long before they see Zarathustra. Little's the difference, 78 percent of them can't remember their congressman's name two months after they vote for him.

Then there is the educated voter. This patriot knows much about each candidate and what he stands for. If none of it, consciously or unconsciously, conflicts with his religion, his business, his color, his place of birth, or a recent zoning decision in his neighborhood, he will, with no equivocation, vote for the best candidate.

We finally come to the elite group of academics, intellectuals, and opinion molders who make a career of voting. Hard, cold facts are their concern, as they dissect each issue and candidate like an entomologist his earthworms. They know the character, commitment, and record of each candidate on everything from the test ban to abortion. But when they themselves are dissected, we find they only differ from the educated voter (and even the Middle American) in that they have the facility and intellect to speciously and articulately defend every ethnic, religious, financial, and intuitive interest and bias they are heirs to.

So what are little voters made of? Hardly sugar and spice and everything nice; they're sort of dull and unethical and somewhat pathetical. If the voter is truly the "last best hope," with what we know of his functioning types—let us pray. But even if miracles happen and somewhere, somehow, there are individuals and subgroups that are everything our Founding Fathers meant them to be, they would still be slim pickings. As of now, those rare birds are undetectable with the means at hand. We have met the voter—and he is us.

Love Thy Leader As Thyself

It's a miracle that two such opposites as leader and follower have existed so peacefully under one political roof without mutual genocide. The answer is simple—they haven't; there have been only superficial and temporary truces. Beneath the surface, they are at it hammer and tong, alternating periods of love and hate in a constant state of flux, though there is no question of who is fluxed more over a period of time.

If there are mixed feelings, they are more mixed for the voter than for the politician. For though the follower is deeply suspicious that every cupidity, stupidity, and incompetence is being visited upon him by the one he voted for (or against), he still instinctively acts with respect and awe, like any dutiful penguin, toward his leader. The leader is different. Deep in his subconscious, he has never forgiven his former serfs and vassals for their uppity action in wresting inherited power from him and making him work to get it back. And he can hardly keep from showing it.

It may not be that obvious to the average voter, but if he'd ever stop to figure out how little he gets out of his vote, he'd realize he couldn't be much worse off as a GNV. To get in touch with an official once elected usually takes about three years and nine months (only three years if one is a large contributor). The communication is through a telephone operator, followed by a form letter reply, on practically any subject. Congressional favors are talked about, but only for one's family, and legitimate gripes are out of the question. It's just as easy to get an audience with the Pope as with a congressman, with fewer blessings accrued from the latter—if the miracle happens at all.

After being told about how much power the voter has, he finds it a little hard to put his finger on exactly what this power is. The only time the feel of it comes over him is in the voting booth—but that lasts only a minute or two. If he attempts to hold the official to his campaign promises, the voter is avoided and shunned like some kind of pariah and is made to feel ashamed for even bringing the subject up. The voter *may be* much better off than when he didn't have that vote—it's just not obvious how. If it weren't drummed into him day in and day out how important he is, he wouldn't feel so psychologically castrated.

Still, this voter, the most adaptable follower of any species on earth, doesn't let his uneasiness keep him down. Just as the demands of survival dictated the evolvement of the opposing thumb and forefinger and man's upright posture, so psychological defense mechanisms popped up to save the voter's security—and his sanity.

Topless—and Bottoms Up

For hope to still spring eternal in the breasts of these billions of voters in search of a Utopia takes a special kind of self-lobotomy, inducing the most complete form of chronic amnesia known as psychiatric annals. Even as his short-term memory has complete recall for every little personal affront or promise by a politician, he has a disremembrance of senile proportions for those epoch public commitments. How else could he bear up under "the war to end wars" and "peace in our time" repeated over and over again by politicians from Pericles to Chamberlain and hailed in each generation as something new, and hopeful? Woodrow Wilson was elected on the slogan "He kept us out of war"—and five months later he declared it.

This is not the worst of it, however. The unconscious psychologic self-ruse at the same time unwittingly contributes to the delinquency of those same leaders. To the voter's detriment, with malice aforethought, the leader depends on this memory lapse—and promises ever more extravagantly as he leads his lemmings to the brink.

The other skin- and mind-saver in the voter's survival kit is his humility. We watch the hilarious antics of a hamadryas baboon unctuously presenting his rainbow-hued rear end to his chief in an act of humble contrition, yet we fail to connect this with the act of genuflecting and kissing a bishop's (as political as any human alpha) ring, done in all reverence and solemnity. Humility is no disgrace, but followers (voters) live up to some long-past instinctual convenant to love, honor, and obey till death do they part that's beyond self-abasement. Captains of industry and even blood brothers automatically show a fawning servility in the presence of power—as witness how the former Supreme Court justice, Abe Fortas, and the former secretary of defense, Clark Clifford, behaved in the presence of their close friend, LBJ. It's as automatic as a knee jerk.

In a further self-denigrating gesture (totally uncalled for), voters add self-insult to kowtow by guaranteeing to provide their leaders with all the accouterments and luxuries they quickly become accustomed to. So if that sanity-saving memory lapse doesn't operate to help the constituent to forget if not forgive, at least his subservient reflexes will help soften the blow, reduce the punishment, and save his skin.

Pragmatics for the Dogmatics

One of the first laws of politico-dynamics, as in evolution, is: "If it's necessary, do it." We always get back to that old, overworked word synonymous with politics and the unenlightened voters—pragmatism. When Hitler needed time, he was pragmatic, he gave a bear hug to his deadly enemy, Stalin; when George McGovern needed the support of the pros, he was pragmatic, he went to LBJ and Mayor Daley, two of his punching bags to the nomination; and when Teddy Kennedy became imbued with the Spirit of '76, he sat pragmatically on the same platform with George Wallace, his dead brother's *bête noir*. Pragmatism is a useful thing. There's no better excuse for any mean, corrupt, or unsuccessful trick a politician has ever pulled.

To the voter, it's even more. Pragmatism is his be-all and end-all. Without it, he'd be even less than he is—if that is possible. After all, what is more pragmatic than seeking that in which there is safety and security—numbers? The voter learned from his atavars, the insects, that he is nothing unless there are lots of him. For way back then, it was *en masse* or *en morte*— and he took the pragmatic route after one thought of the alternative.

Yet, knowing this, our Founding Fathers with straight faces still regaled the voter with another grim fairy tale of our folk hero, our golden calf—the individual. (As FDR put it, he liked nothing better than rugged individualists—as long as they conformed.) Even as a follower is told what a great individualist he is, he knows he's better off in a crowd, an ethnic group, a party no different from the colony his little ant ancestors would never think of leaving. And just like his insect relatives, as an individual he is helpless, spending a lifetime running in circles to avoid a heavy foot; but as part of an ant army, one species undistinguishable, he can defoliate a jungle.

The Adversity of Diversity

Quantity, not quality; sameness, not difference, makes the voter's world go round. As much as every little voter has his Walter Mitty dreams and would love to poke his receding forehead and prognathus jaw above the crowd for one delirious moment, it's much less risky being a dues-paying member of Voters Anonymous. Anonymity is not only the great security blanket, the great leveler, but, like the lever, if used properly it can lift the world. It was used properly and as predicted, "the unheard of, the anonymous inherited the earth." But there was a problem—after they got it, they didn't know what to do with it.

But Boss Crump in Tennessee and Boss Hague in Jersey City did—and their political heirs still do. They knew what anonymity could do—it bred unanimity, which is what piles up pluralities and majorities. What else was there to know? Honey Fitz said it all when he told his workers not to bother with the Cabots and the Lodges: "There ain't enough of 'em, and what there are can't be trusted to vote like they should." He cherished those look-alike, feel-alike, act-alike Irishmen who voted as if only one horny hand X-ed those ballots.

If someone had told Hague or Crump or Tweed, or anyone else who knew about the workings of politics, that a democracy thrives on diversity, he'd have had him committed. It's like telling the house-mother of the Vestal Virgins that Hugh Hefner would make a marvelous companion.

There can be no flies in the ointment. If an unguent is to render its soothing balm, it must be silky, smooth, with no strange insects stuck in it. The unsame, the independent, the mavericks of the New (or Old) Politics are gingerly picked out with thumb and forefinger, their wings plucked off, never to mess up another healing salve.

Diversity? That's what gave the Republicans Barry Goldwater in 1964 and the Democrats McGovern in 1972. Hubert Humphrey learned about the democracy of diversity firsthand in 1968 as the diverse academics, intellectuals, and Wallacites—Democrats all—pulled out the stops, each in his own direction, and blew a registered national majority and a presidency.

Morality Quo-Un-Quo

It is said that a democracy rests on the voter's morality, loyalty, and innate goodness and reason. If so, we can put the red, white, and blue carnations on its grave every Tuesday after the first Monday in November. For even in the first instance, if there were a voter escutcheon, it must be symbolized by none other than the crossed and outstretched palm under a fluffy field of greenbacks and the Latin credo lettered in fine old English: "*Quid pro Quo*" (What's in it for me?). When the voter pulls the curtain, crosses himself in a ballotlike X, bows his head, recites his *Quid pro* catechism, pleas for guidance, and opens his eyes, he will without fail pull the lever in self-interest— enlightened or otherwise. It's not that the voter isn't moral and religious, it's only that he has a stronger attachment to the faith of the "quo." The pork barrel is a smelly container only when the other guys get the rivers and harbors windfall. And woe to the politician who doesn't provide the carrion—he becomes it.

The moral Bostonians received Mayor Curley back into office with open arms from his penitentiary campaign headquarters, for the good mayor was a *quo* sharer. The gentle voter in Texas (in 1971) overwhelmingly put Congressman John Dowdy back in his hard-earned seat though he was indicted before election not only of perjury, conspiracy, and bribery, but declared mentally unfit to stand trial at that time by government psychiatrists. But how could old John be amoral when he had always done so well by his constituency? (Even his colleagues didn't think he was unfit, as they forthrightly returned him to his committee chairmanship.)

There are hundreds of such examples of moral rectitude devoted to the *quo*. Pendergast (Truman's old boss) was suspected of dipping into the Missouri till, but Harry stood by him. Mayors Jimmy Walker and Bill O'Dwyer in New York were the toasts of the electorate even as they stole them blind. And Congressman Cornelius Gallagher of New Jersey was alleged in a *Life* magazine article (which he disputed) to have had the corpse of a minor gangster mouldering in his cellar as he handily won his seat back. It takes more than just a few little indiscretions to shake a voter's faith in an incumbent—if he's a revenue sharer.

Loyalty—It Suffered in Translation

So much for morality. As to loyalty, as Watergate has amply proven, it is no myth in government. Cabinet members, captains of industry, attorney generals, the FBI, and even account executives—all simple folk—went down the line and some of them allegedly even perjured and burgled for their chief. Loyalty in politics (if immunity is not offered) is no sometime thing, there is an honor (or sorts) among thieves except when plea-bargaining. As Konrad Lorenz has shown, it can be carried a little too far and end up with a "dangerous barbarian splitting your skull with the clearest possible conscience."

Loyalty occasionally suffers in translation from its perfection in the dog, the cat, and even Elsa the lioness. For humans, it is sometimes tough to be loyal and pragmatic at the same time. Though a voter rarely shifts his allegiance (about 15 to 20 percent of the time), when he does, it's usually for good and enlightened reasons. For instance, if the bandwagon going in the opposite direction is much bigger, richer, and better than the one he's on, that's reason enough.

The Democratic pros for Nixon in 1972 and the Republican pros for Johnson in 1964 were the epitome of loyalty and only bowed to the weight of pique and pragmatics (where does Irv Kovens of *Kickback County*, Maryland go when his own party shuts him out).

True, the proletarian rank and file of labor deserted the Democratic party—for George Wallace in 1968 and for Nixon in 1972. But after forty years of being tied to one party they deserved a little respite and anyway what did McGovern do lately for labor. The black leadership (Coretta King, Jess Jackson, and Julian Bond) would never have left HHH, the champion of their rights, for McGovern, except for a better promise.

Loyalty, however, is no one-way street. The leaders had

better return it, not only in coin, but in kind. Woe to the elected ones who grow different from their elected image—or even grow. The scholarly Senator William Fulbright wasn't elected by quoting Thucydides to his down-country razorbacks. He gave them all the "corn pone" and "you all" they wanted and just about "blue-grassed" them on a Jew's harp. But when he breathed the heady capital atmosphere, his scholarly bent emerged from under the campaign slick and he had visions of instant statesmanship (another term for a self-destructive urge to put the nation above a constituency). The ADA suicide squad encouraged this scholarly Southern liberal (a great catch) to speak out on civil rights and coexistence. But Fulbright's radar caught the message from Little Rock. He scurried back to his "red-eye gravy and grits" integration policy, which he hasn't left since. Now he's not only against foreign aid, Israel, and bussing but his ADA rating in 1968 plummeted to 16—somewhere around Strom's.

The other two voter attributes necessary for a successful democracy—reason and innate goodness—are too remote to be discussed with either goodness or reason. If they were extant, this utopia would need no democracy to mess it up. As Ibsen put it, "the most dangerous enemy to truth and freedom is the majority."

The Temperamental Slug

Contrary to all accounts, the voter isn't 100 percent slug —which accounts for that 15 percent of the time when he becomes disloyal and malcontent. It's really not so much that he disagrees on the issues as he just gets bored with his own phlegm. The first hint of this choler is frequently a catchy phrase—"It's time for a change" or "Throw the rascals out." With it comes a spate of angina pectoris and Excedrin headaches for the incumbent. When he hears that old refrain, he battens down the hatches, throws the bolts, and prepares for the worst. It's the first harbinger of a long, hard winter.

The rarest political qualities—experience, wisdom, and a decent record—may get buried in the snows of simple voter whimsy. The perservering four-term senator, Margaret Chase

Smith, fell before a shiny, bright candidate of no special com-
petence and for no special reason. When the voter's dander is
up, the glisten of a "shiny bright" catches his rheumy eye.

It doesn't take much glisten, sometimes only a face, a physique, a drive, and a few talk shows. A spanking "new," six-foot,
three-inch John Lindsay, with late-show credentials, was a
cinch in New York City, beating phalanges of solid pedestrian-
type Republicans and Democrats alike. Movie star Ronald
Reagan, with tall-in-the-saddle Class B horse opera identification,
galloped past the sagging-jawed, tried-and-true speaker of the California House, Jess Unruh, into the statehouse (and maybe—who
knows?—into the hearts of his countrymen).

Don't Knock a Winner

With all his basic flaws and other special capacities to misjudge,
and mismanage, himself, the voter has survived the burdens of
these few hundred years of democracy. And in the great game of
evolution, one doesn't knock a survivor. His durability comes not
from the system, but despite it—he'll weather it as he did slavery
and feudalism. As usual, the follower opts for security and leaves
the frivolous identity revels and excitement wallowings to his
leaders. The system hasn't hurt the voter, but neither has he hurt
it. Which is not to say that eventually they won't both go down
together. It's just too bad that what our Forefathers brought
forth upon this continent and the ordinary follower weren't
made for each other.

Voter character obviously hasn't speeded up the processes of
democracy, but at least it hasn't detracted from its noble purpose
—though purpose may be all that is left of it. If time holds out,
it is conceivable that the persistence of the voter could drag the
system down to his level. Then a sort of compatability will result. But our present far-fetched hope that the follower will
learn to live up to the system takes the same faith and vision
as belief in the Second Coming. A new voter mutant is the
other possibility, but just as long a shot.

V

Ego Genetics—
The Political Id

(*The Importance of Being Important*)

The quest for immortality is the condition of a dead man who doesn't
believe he is dead.

—H. L. MENCKEN

Security is always the first of three basic psychologic needs in
any mentally stable animal or man. Identity and excitement
come a poor second and third. But not with the politician—it's
identity all the way. He would *pay any price, bear any burden,*
and *meet any hardship* for a paragraph in *Time* or a three-
column picture in *News of the Week in Review*. And this is
only a clue to his identity mania. For him, recognition begins
almost at birth but goes even beyond the churchyard epitaph.
His underlying passion is not only to be known, but to be known
by everyone, everywhere, forever. For in the politician's re-
strained immodesty, it is inconceivable that those great deeds
associated with his calling be interred with his bones. He feels
it is only historical justice that his mortal status be suitably
monumented for eternity.

This is not an unreasonable conceit, for the insatiable identity
urge of politicians is not a conscious drive but an instinct bred in
the genes, built into the fiber, and circulating in the vessels.
Though power is the ultimate goal and identification only the
means, politicians frequently confuse them, becoming so en-

tranced with the colors of the rainbow they overshoot the pot of gold.

The unabashed lust to be known overrides not only political common sense, but even the survival instinct. If Lyndon Johnson or Ike Eisenhower thought twice about their health or longevity after major heart attacks and surgery, they didn't show it, continuing in a job that takes the strength of a water buffalo, the persistence of a dung beetle, and the staying power of a Galápagos tortoise. It eventually helped do them in. Teddy Kennedy still takes the identity risk his two brothers were buried for, as George Wallace risks quadriplegia. And though the famous and glamorous avoid crowds, the politician still seeks them out even in this era of mayhem.

There could be no sane rationale for a nice Waspish boy like John Lindsay, who already had everything, masochistically working the ethnic grass roots on the sidewalks of New York, and foregoing the adoration of Washington's toney "F" Street club on those Tuesday-to-Thursday Capitol work weeks. Why else would he have risked his safe Silk Stocking congressional district and his beautiful Southamptonites on those four-day weekends to sweat around the clock walking the ghettos (as they went up in flames), confronting rabid cab drivers, vicious teacher unions, a violent subway system, a corrupt police, and an uncontrollable City Council? Could it all be made worthwhile by a front-page photo in the *Daily News*, triumphantly settling a garbage strike? To John Lindsay it could and was.

The Identity Junky

This identity bug in the political psyche enlarges into weird shapes and sizes at different political levels. At the top it becomes a giant Kafkaesque roach. Roosevelt, de Gaulle, and Hitler would settle for nothing less than immortal worship, in eternal flame, print, and song. On the other hand, a ward heeler in East Milwaukee is satisfied that his deeds and earthy eccentricities be passed along by word of mouth in the beery tavern accolade, "They don't make them like that anymore." To a governor, it may be bronze plaques on bridges and roads; to a secretary of the treasury, his signature on a zillion-dollar bill; to

the chairman of the House Subcommittee on Labor and Education, his name chiseled in school cornerstones up and down the
land. Even George McGovern would not settle for less than a
paragraph or two in the history books (with the hope that the
gory details be forgotten).

We all have some of this identity suet clogging our cerebral
vessels, but who else makes a career of it? We all know that
there's just no one else on earth exactly like us and that we
differ a scintilla here or there from our fellow termite in the
swarm. So what? We may try to show it by batting a ball, blowing a horn, or wearing a fringed buckskin jerkin and a beaded
headband. Surely no one can blame us if before our remains are
cached away we try to show for one second in time that we are
not stamped from the same dye as everyone else. Even the
peacock shows he's different from the goose by spreading his
plumage; and the fiddler crab tries to demonstrate his superiority
by waving his one huge claw above the other claws in his crowd
as if to say, "Here I am—there's nobody better than me." But
whether it's Park Avenue or a beach full of crabs, if no one
looks, it's not a tragedy—except to politicians. For they who
practice the noble art, obscurity is not just limbo—it's purgatory.
Dante's Seventh Circle of Hell must have anonymity as one of
its worst punishments for politicians (strangely enough, the
opposite—anonymity—is the life and breath of the follower).

An unidentified politician is a nonesuch, and who knows it
better than the part of that little gene grasping for more space,
larger headlines, and bigger crowds? In moderation, seeking
recognition is not a vice, but what politician practices moderation? As Adlai Stevenson said, "Listen to your introductions and
read your publicity but don't inhale either." No doubt it's
hazardous to political health. Arthur Goldberg, former Supreme
Court justice, did and still does inhale his notices, and look
where he is now. He lost his place on the Supreme Bench
(when LBJ flattered him into taking the UN job so he could
give the seat on the Court to Fortas) and then lost the
gubernatorial race in New York. But the most objective of
politicians (objective politicians?) sops up the adulation and
applause to his capacity, for he knows it's all absolutely true and
deserved. Even the taciturn, indifferent, pipe-smoking Senate

majority leader comes alive (if you can call it that) when his namesake, the "mike," is pushed under his nose.

If the pol doesn't heed Adlai's advice and inhales, aspirates, imbibes, or absorbs the stuff in moderation, both for his identity kick and to get him where he's going, it can't hurt too much. To him, public attention is coke, LSD, uppers, and downers rolled into one great trip, taken without a prescription and needing no pushers. He's in trouble only when the monkey's on his back and he mainlines it, building tolerance, the highs getting shorter. The more he gets, the more he wants. Then he'll beg, bribe, or pander for his daily fix, whether a squib in the *Times* or a front-page picture in the *Weekly Picayune*. Spiro Agnew (a real Iden-junky) only ten years ago was pleased as punch at a headline in the blurry-inked Baltimore County weekly *The Jeffersonian*. But he reached a point where he turned down everything but network prime time. Though it was more than identity that caused his premature passing, in his final throes he would have been better off not being a household word.

Political deaths from publicity OD fill the post-election obits. That young hopeful Senator Fred Harris came to the Capitol with Oklahoma dirt still between his toes and died (politically) a few years later in his McLean rancher abandoned by PR and press, the needle still deep in his vein. Like a Phoenix he had risen—suddenly a U.S. senator, fresh country-style spokesman for the American Indian, the poor, and the black, appointed executive director of the famous Kerner Commission by President Johnson and then chairman of the Democratic National Committee. Up, up, and away.

The New York Review and *The New Republic* touted him as the greatest civil rights advocate since HHH. He believed it—all of it. He jumped on presidential bandwagons, looked for a vice presidential opening, and was almost as regular on the *Today* show and *Meet the Press* as Barbara Walters and Larry Spivak. More reporters than constituents crowded his office, and more network celebrities than friends his home. Ribbon cutting, cornerstone laying, and speeches from coast to coast took priority over fence mending, party caucuses, and roll call votes on (Oklahoma) oil depletion allowances. His "white racism" became a household word not only in New York and Boston (and here comes the rub), but from Tulsa to the panhandle as well. He was so sincere and convincing that even the old red-neck segregationists who backed him began to reckon he believed what he was saying. He was at once both a publicity-built national figure and a publicity-shredded local calamity. He died by the identity sword (without even a shot at running again) as he lived by it—too anemic to defend his seat. R.I.P. Fred Harris.

Don't Color It (All) Green—or Gold

Even though to the minds of the great unwashed corruption in politics is all for money nothing could be farther from the truth. It's recognition and status that's the root of all political evil—money is only second. Not that the politician is averse to fattening his own purse but he lovingly counts his political *due bills* and popularity like no Shylock ever poured over coin of the realm. The politician wouldn't trade a *Meet The Press* glimpse of himself for all the contents of a loaded Brinks truck. Some, of course, aren't loathe to use their power and popularity for that olive-green tender (as Baltimore showed there is more to be made in a County seat then in a Senate committee chair). A color more dear to the smarter and more prudent politician's heart on the upper rungs is somewhere in between—sort of rosey flush of success at the polls blended with the *green* and *gold* into a Tiffany-like pinkish-chartreuse.

With fifty million dollars gushing through the Watergate sluices, only the usual petty-cash larcenies occurred. The prototype of the fat-cat politician originates not so much with the real political animal, but with the short-term pretenders low on the ladder who neither know power nor how to keep it. An amateur like Agnew—misplaced from the beginning—showed no political finesse in his business transactions—a precinct captain would have been ashamed of his amateurish maneuverings.

Even the behaviorists and social psychologists are on the wrong track with their "reinforcement" (the social psychologist's term for reward or loot as a political motive). As René Dubos stated, "The lust for political power independent of any desire for financial or material reward has the same prototypes in animal behavior." If the social scientists would only look back to their animal heritage, they would see the identity lust as strong in the blowfish as in the candidate. The chief baboon lets an insistent young female in heat cool her "heels" until he imbibes all of the carefully subservient grooming worship of each and every one of his troop. A young punk chimpanzee leader, even if hungry, steals a ripe banana from under the chief alpha's nose only to grandstand it and toss it aside, bowing low to the hooting plaudits of his peers.

If the "reinforcers" had just a hint of the anguish, travail, and ignominy a politician goes through for that *itch to be known*, they'd realize even the golden carrot of pure power can't really sate the identity appetite. Nelson Rockefeller (with a friend at Chase Manhattan) needs security and power like he needs a dime bank. Yet in seeking the limelight and public love and acclaim, he risks everything—comfort, a piece of his fortune, and even life itself. This scion of wealth and might resents not one hour spent in a sleazy two-bit bar in the Village hammering out a deal with cauliflower-eared ward bosses and Brooklyn borough lieutenants for a couple of thousand more ballot tallies and a personal slap on the back by the regulars downing their red-eye —just to prove how much he's loved. Finishing at 2 A.M. (the political witching hour), he has to look forward to nothing less gruesome than a 6 A.M. wakeup for a local TV show three hundred miles away in freezing Albany, where another couple of thousand people (he knows not and cares little about) will add their imprimatur to his need for acclaim. For this, he will miss a sophisticated Park Avenue dinner party with friends and celebrities and a heavenly shower next noon from gold-plated faucets.

Behaviorists or no, this kind of drive (or mania) couldn't be learned by promises of Eden. It's born in the womb, usually with no more than one to a family. Other than the Kennedys, the siblings of presidents or aspiring candidates (Nixon, Lyndon Johnson, George McGovern, or Hubert Humphrey) hide rather than seek it out.

The Excitement Bonus

Besides the number 1 (recognition) and the number 2 (security) needs of politicians, there is a third psychologic need of stimulation or excitement. Other than the most bizarre type of politician like Eugene McCarthy, boredom is a rare political affliction. For in the identity mix, the politician gets a freebie of stimulation thrown in. Recognition and power are not only exciting in themselves, they are also exciting in the getting. As Eisenhower admitted, no military victory (Rockefeller would agree that no financial coup) could provoke the adrenals like an election-night victory. When a politician, with deep humility and in stentorian tones, accepts the concession of his rival, he is euphorically thinking that thirty thousand or thirty million people are in love with him.

In the patas monkey leader, the acclaim of his troop even produces a physiologic response—his scrotum turns an electric blue. This may also be true of human politicians, though even Rowland Evans and Robert Novak haven't yet recorded this phenomenon in their Capitol observations.

After the initial jolt of victory, the winner is dished out smaller daily rations of the same excitement by the little man—in a restaurant, on the street, or at the airport. These doses make the politician's heart pound and his eyes glisten. But there is a built-in escalator of rising expectations. Though recognition blossoms more with each success, the need for it is never quite requited. The feed salesman is never the same after winning that first campaign for county clerk. It's like the fierce arrogance engendered in the feisty young chimpanzee by the bare-fanged screeching cheers of his admirers after he's led his first successful foray into strange territory. The taste of undue deference, the lift of new respect from the Main Street barber or drugstore cashier, is heavy stuff. He then experiences the feeling of Julius Caesar or Ike Eisenhower passing through the Arc de Triomphe, even as the political gene sits back confidently knowing this politician is only getting the due she allows him.

Ego Currents and Electoral Juices

From the first political success the ego currents of the political brain are switched on and the electoral juices begin to flow. The beauty (or tragedy) of it is that though it never climaxes, the politician never gets tired of it. Every night is election night. He must constantly question: "Mirror, mirror—who's superior to them all?" And he's out there making sure. If there's doubt, he'll do something about it. Doing something about it means beating the bushes for more identity. Somehow this is not conducive to the tranquility one equates with statesmen. Tranquility? Politicians can tolerate only short bursts of it. But we're talking about excitement. Who needs tranquility? Paradoxically, even though the politician is a loner, it's people that count with him, more and more of them. And if he's at home—no people; if he's asleep—no people; if he's in a study—no people. How can he tell he is what he knows he is without meetings, banquets, rallies, and conventions?

Poll any political wife and the lament is standard "Life with Father" during recess, vacation, or their semi-annual evening at home, is life with a caged lion.

To the layman, not all political excitement seems all that exciting. There must be something politicians feel that we don't. But how can we put ourselves in the politician's shoes, how can we possibly fathom the esoteric stimulation of a tavern full of boozy party faithfuls?

Even more of a mystery to the simple voter mind is that Rhodes Scholars and Phi Beta Kappas like Congressman John Brademas of Indiana and Speaker Carl Albert can glow in the enjoyment of that most soporific of political institutions—the testimonial or fund-raising dinner. These dulling menaces to both the mind and the digestive tract, graced by those who must be seen or "papered," are like a shot of B_{12} to even the (rare) political intellectual. Al Smith once told his doctor while flat in bed in the hospital that there was no illness, depression, or reversal he'd ever had that couldn't be soothed or cured by a foot-stomping, hell-raising political rally. Even the dozing political octogenarian's jowls are creased by beatific smiles during the main address.

This enigma is explained by the beneficent politician in one of those biblical quotes they so like to be caught using: "It's better to give than to receive." If politicians are what they think they are (which they don't doubt), what more golden gift can they give us than a part of themselves (which is about all they ever give)? If the gospel premises are valid, so is the explanation.

The Specter of "Out"

But we haven't explored the dark side of the identity moon. The specter of "out" and anonymity lurks in every elected official's mind. The thought of rejection by their loved ones is unbearable in view of the fact that it is immediately public knowledge—with no possible excuse, for there is no such thing as real voluntary political retirement. When LBJ chose not to run to prevent dividing the nation, he was only saying "Ah think ah can't win." As lazy as Senator Eugene McCarthy is, and his protests notwithstanding, nothing could have pried him loose from his Senate seat but a taste of that presidential identity elixir. After his 1968 ego fiasco, nothing could satisfy him but more of the same and it wasn't in the Senate. He's tried about everything since, from poetry to publishing, and it looks like he'll now settle for a lesser stake, even a seat in the House, for that lifeblood—the limelight. Even after twenty-four reruns, octogenarian Congressman Manny Celler fought like fury in a last-ditch gasp to keep not only his power, but also his place in the sun. Senator Mundt of South Dakota grimly hung on for two years though felled speechless and senseless by a stroke. When one gets acclimated to the rarefied recognition atmosphere, one becomes short of breath at sea level.

If it were not for the compassionate, and genetically compatible) electorate that sends the incumbent back 80 percent of the time, St. Elizabeth's, the Federal Psychiatric Institute near Washington, would be loaded with ex–elected officials with catatonic withdrawal syndromes. It first hits home to these lost leaders with a drop in the RQ (recognition quotient). When six months after the votes are counted, the man in the street asks "Congressman Who?"; the postman hardly rings once with those deeply embossed embassy invitations; speaking engagements dry up and requests for interviews are no more, it's a sad day in Polville. Unofficialdom is a sorry state of helpless oblivion, intolerable to the once-glorified. These lost leaders lurk around the fringes of power cadging a line or two from a sympathetic reporter who was once their trusted "leak line," or at best wind up under the *Newsweek* epitaph "Where Are They Now"—medicine barely strong enough to stop the nausea or cramps.

The political loser suddenly finds that catering to a kooky tax nut or reading letters from a senile Medicare patient about how his enemas were not administered by a qualified M.D. or even absorbing the bitter calumny of paranoid reporters is life and breath compared to anonymity. Speaking at a second cousin's family reunion becomes a golden opportunity. Political office at any level is a little oxygen—a bit of identity.

Ask Claude Pepper, a former senior U.S. senator (who lost his seat seniority and prestige after the age of fifty), if he'd rather be among the grateful dead in Florida with his lucrative law practice at seventy-one or returning as he later did as a freshman to the House of Representatives. Just the thought of losing prods a politician to plod that recognition treadmill harder and longer. It's out front or out period. He must ply his name and fame with no surcease and with the same popularity-contest mentality of Zsa Zsa Gabor or John Wayne. If he stands still, he's a goner. Here he is only imitating the bull elephant, as he must periodically trumpet his dominance, or the gorilla, as he thumps out his ego reminder to the rest of the troop.

The Divine Right of Genes

So a politician's life is not an easy one. Since the Magna Carta put the Divine Right of Kings to rest and the French Revolution kiboshed the inherited throne, the leadership gene has been on its own, competing in the marketplace. The gene knows it must live with this, but accepts it reluctantly.

This majority-rule business is all right, but if you know you're the best, why have to prove it every two, four, or six years? The politician sighs, nostalgically dreaming of the good old days when his geneologic ancestors were handed their power and status at birth on a silver platter, gold spoon and all.

However, if these are the new rules and you're on the shelf *(For Sale)*, why *hide your light under a bushel?* Moderation not being a politician's strong suit, he will go the limit. It pays to advertise and he does so for love, affection—and votes.

In the final analysis, though, it's not really a selfish desire —it's for a greater cause. It's not just conceit or egomania, he *knows* that if his image persists, his special mix of genes, his nobility of purpose, his capacity and creativity will be remembered and taken as an example and probably bode a better world. In any event, he couldn't do differently if he wanted to.

VI

Hen House Politics

(*The Peck is Mightier Than . . .*)

The so-called pecking order is the principle of organization without which a political life can't develop. Under this everyone knows which one is stronger and which weaker than himself so that everyone can retreat from the stronger and expect submission from the weaker if they should get in each other's way.

—KONRAD LORENZ, *On Aggression*

There is no organization effective or ineffective that is run by equality, liberty, fraternity, or a committee. If there is an organization, there is a pecking order with few at the top and many at the bottom. And the pecking order is as rigid at 1600 Pennsylvania Avenue as in any barnyard. When the man in the Oval Office sniffles, the Marine band strikes up "Ruffles and Flourishes," the administrative assistants get shaking chilblains, and the White House guard at the West Gate comes down with double pneumonia. As soon as the news got out that John Kennedy was fed up with State Department ineptitude and had likened it to a "bowl of jelly," it began to shake like one. Dean Rusk's Georgia drawl become as clipped as a drill sergeant's command, Foggy Bottom became an incandescent beehive, and the furled umbrellas of the Foreign Service officers were all in a row each and every morning at precisely 7:30 A.M. and not disturbed till the wee hours.

Schrelderup-Ebbe, the eminent psychologist who first described the classic pecking order in the hen house, could have studied the Pentagon or the Bureau of the Budget with identical results. On whatever roost—Aphid's, Ape's, or Politician's—the "head cock" rules. When he is dissatisfied, irritated, has a splitting headache, or is just hungover, he will give a snarling peck to his second in command that is felt down to the bottom rung. The subordinate pecks back at his peril. His only emotional release is to peck out at the nearest one lower in rank. The hen on the bottom rung will get a peck from the next to the lowest, never know why, and had better not question it.

Gentlemen's Agreement

At each level, the underling, though taking his pecks like a man, has an innate compulsion to drive higher—as high as he can go. From the peanut brain under the red coxcomb to the (sometimes) complicated cortex under the Homburg, the same Adlerian psychology of the "push upward" is at work. Professor Adler, one of the many fathers of psychiatry, put this down as a basic human instinct. Each level casts a longing eye at his superior (dodging the droppings from above) and a wary one at his ambitious inferior as he drops at will. But like water, politicians seek their own level. A push here, a break there, a death, a vacancy, or a gerrymander may temporarily carry a politician beyond his rightful niche, but sooner or later he settles—rarely above the level his genes have set. Though complaining every inch of the way of the ill-fortune and adversity that have put him where he is, in his heart he knows it's right.

This system has been around ever since the political chickens first came home to roost. It's lasted only because it works. Like all other evolutionary successes from the hive to the herd, it was created for survival. A chicken or a baboon will battle his way up every rung of the way, but once it's decided who belongs where, there is a gentlemen's agreement to stay put. The losers either settle down or get out, and peace and order reign over the hen house. Accepting fate lessens conflict in a wolf pack, an elephant herd, or the West Wing of the White House. In the human hierarchy, however, though the ancient pecking order is still at work, it doesn't function as smoothly—especially in a democracy where it's been drummed into each hen that "it ain't necessarily so," which results in delusions of grandeur, fewer gentlemen's agreements, harder losers, and more problems.

Just as this automatic arrangement for peace and tranquility began early in history, it starts early in life: It is a drive apparent in any litter from pigs to politicians. No sooner are they born when one (usually a male) strikes out for the fullest teat, gets there first, and rules the brood from then on—first one in is a politician. *And by their striving ye shall know them:* on the manure pile, in the nursery, and in the local feed salesman as he wins his first campaign for county clerk with covert dreams of the Capitol cloakroom. It is a rare city councilman who isn't confident he could handle the statehouse better; and not one of the fifty at the Governors' Conference or the hundred on the Senate floor doesn't secretly feel that "he's the one."

The Golden Roost

What better insight into the vicissitudes of the political pecking order than the roost of the White House itself. Like Mount Everest, it's climbed because it's there. Eggs are laid (some of them very large indeed), nests are guarded (and padded), heights are reached, and depths plumbed (without the benefit of the "trade").

Every four years on January 20, the old manure is pitchforked out, the nests are limed and sprayed, and a new flock moves in. Each of the high betas (those directly under the head rooster), chosen by the one and only high alpha (the chief cock himself), is placed on the rung he supposedly fits. Early on, it's a happy hen house. Chromosomes are temporarily satisfied by the deference, the pomp and panoply, the aura of power, and the sense of history at the White House, everyone is in thrall.

But not for long, because the aura of, and the sense of, is never enough for betas. The genes soon begin to fidget, compelling each aide to jockey for that warm spot under the alpha's downy wing (or shadowy jaw). Since there's little room there for more than one or two, push comes to shove and the settling in and dropping out begins. The few on that top rung mean to stay there. Their guard is up day and night (their secretaries alerted) to allow only a select few to penetrate to the head cock. Finch, Hickel, and Rogers, all high-ranking cabineteers and close to RMN, knew when they'd gone as far as they could and stopped beating their beaks against the palace wall. The Connallys, Schultzes, and Lairds come and go, but the palace guard goes on forever (until Watergate).

As it's said, "When they have the body, they've got it all." And in protecting that body, they've got the inside—the power—and use it. There are a few, if any, dodges, tricks, and subterfuges of their position they don't use, and what's more, no one dares question their means. They keep presidential friends, fat cats, confidants, and even relatives beholden to them. JFK's mother, Lyndon Johnson's and Richard Nixon's brothers, and Hubert Humphrey's sister complained bitterly of not being able to get an appointment or even a call through. Watergate showed us that the palace guard was well dug-in. Nixon would have only given up Rebozo or San Clemente more reluctantly than he did Haldeman and Ehrlichman.

Fair is Fowl

As Watergate also showed, though *they* may have had the body, only "*one*" really had it. Once the Pennsylvania Avenue Beta Boys' Choir got offkey, each singing his own little tune to the Ervin Committee, it all hung out—not unlike any other animal herd. H. R. (Bob) Haldeman and his combined axeman and lint brusher John Ehrlichman had been locked in silent but deadly battle with Martha's husband John like stags with antlers entwined, almost since the inaugural. It was obvious that H. R. (Bob) came out as the true high cock of that dung heap.

But if we hark back to the barnyard dung heap, there's nothing unexpected about this. It's ever thus in every regime, and may last years, bloody and exciting enough for a Roman Coliseum (except for the lack of anything Christian or leonine about it). Under the guise of a paper-thin surface camaraderie, the betas deliver a metaphorical gouge here, a chop or a jab there, or a razor-edged derogatory whisper. They peck away with no letup, not only to get up on top, but to stay there —alone, all alone. Near the end of the first term it gets rougher and less subtle, and stiletto-proof turtlenecks are the uniform of the day.

This is not to say that if there is the slightest move by any outlander to get through they don't all band together in a solid phalanx, the wont of any palace guard. The high-rungers not only reinforce the sterile zone already set up around the president, protecting that chief cock (precautions of which he is aware), but they also add to their own protection and security in the process. There's an old axiom from Daugherty, President Harding's mentor and keeper: "To stay on top, keep him cloistered, content, and uncontaminated from contact and climbers." When the emergency is over, as if an all-clear has been sounded, they again go at each other hammer and tong.

This system occasionally results in a happy irony. Agnew and some of the other higher-ups, if not as clean as a hound's tooth, were well rabbit-footed during the Watergate mess. By the grace of God and the pecking order, they were "caper"-free. As it's now been shown, there were few who were chosen who didn't serve—both the president and possibly time. The J. Walter Thompson beta bunch had no intention of allowing a toe-in to the inner sanctum (the Watergate sewing circle), for the fourth law of chicken-roost dynamics is that anyone privy to presidential secrets is privy to the president himself.

Like gamblers at a cockfight, the entire staff, from cabinet down, maintains a constant vigil at the subtle (and not so subtle) vacillations of power. They have their money (and their rung) riding on one or the other high betas, and you can't tell a player without a scorecard. With each rise and fall (each erection and resurrection), the strength of their cock is assessed and bets are hedged. Their own access or pipeline to the Oval Office and even their jobs hang in the balance. The lowliest omega secretary has her antennae out and leans accordingly. She, too, is attracted to the ambience of power (even by association) and shifts with the current. There's no loyalty like "rung loyalty."

Seen One You've Seen Them All

All White House roost struggles are the same. From the Roosevelt days with Harry Hopkins and Rex Tugwell up to the very present. They all use beak and spur with just as little subtlety and no less rancor. Incumbent high betas of the Nixon regime peck with as jugular an earnestness as the Bill Moyers, the Marvin Watsons, and the Joe Califanos, whose offices protected LBJ like a Maginot Line.

In a typical barnyard scenario in 1966, majordomo Watson and the ambitious next-in-line Califano nudged the fair-haired press secretary ("lak mah own son"), Moyers, out of favor by subtly encouraging him in some very risky maneuvers—which proved to be fatal. LBJ could smell ambition down at the other end of the Mall. It boded a bad trip to second-guess that most raunchy of cocks. Moyers was expeditiously dispatched to civilian status with no paternal blessings, only the usual public amenities observed in any chicken yard. Which left Watson and Califano to put their tough stew-chicken muscles to work, quietly throwing the spurs to each other. The banjo-eyed little Califano, who had wriggled up the hard way from the Pentagon, was no match for Texas-bred Watson. He knew he had reached his peak and wound up as Watson's number 1 flunky, with only the vice president and the assistant cabinet secretaries to peck at. These may sound like some pretty choice targets, but in that roof-high golden dung pile, the vice president has about as little power as (and even less access than) the president's valet.

The All-Purpose Pecking Boy

In a pecking order where there is something for almost everyone, even the lower White House aides take special delight in the all-purpose pecking boy—the vice president. Spiro Agnew was lucky if H. R. (Bob) cleared more than three consecutive alliteratives in one speech (like *wasteful Watergate wampum*), something dear to Spiro's jingle-bent heart, much less allow him within a mile of the 8:15 briefing sessions. If he didn't stay in line and keep his blunt axe dulled, a speech to the

Rural Postmistresses of America would be cancelled and a third assistant postmaster general sent to substitute. Gerald Ford, his successor (whom LBJ diagnosed as a victim of brain softening), with Nixon on top, could well wind up with just cranial jelly holding hands with Spiro in some special vice presidential limbo.

The deference or derision every vice president gets from the president's assistants fluctuates according to favor he holds with the president at any one time. Usually the betas reflect the president's usual indifference toward his second man by niggling actions such as keeping him waiting in their outer offices or telling him "the President's too busy this month." No treatment of this second position was more flagrant, nor more denigrating, than the way Ken O'Donnell (JFK's appointment secretary) handled the proud LBJ, even denying him a cruise with friends on the *Sequoia* on hot Sunday afternoons—until, of course, November of 1963.

On the other hand, there was no more sudden reversal of attitude than that which occurred between March 31 (when Johnson withdrew his candidacy) and April 2, 1968, when Hubert Humphrey (suddenly projected as a presidential candidate) lunched in the staff dining room of the West Wing. Even the Filipino waiters silently serving the bean soup and hamburgers in the low-ceilinged, white-linened basement room were aware of the little drama unfolding. They watched the once crisply haughty Johnson intimates metamorphose into a limp lot bereft of the starch of their alpha, but even worse, bereft of the security, importance, and identification that came from him. Watson, Califano, and John Roche (the Johnson regime intellectual?), all at separate tables, waited impatiently and deferentially for their former pecking boy to finish his coffee. Well liked, but usually only accorded a perfunctory wave from those busy young bantams, HHH purposely dawdled as they perspired, then welcomed them one by one, relishing the switch and aware of both their fears and motives. Every presidential regime and unsuccessful candidate has a large trash heap of leftovers who pick themselves up and brush themselves off, ready to be used again. Many of them from Tommy the Cork (of FDR's day) to the O'Briens, Califanos, Schlesingers, Wirtzs, Galbraiths (even to a Texas Republican) put themselves back on the shelves to be merchandised as bargains for practically any job, to practically any candidate—almost any ideology notwithstanding.

The Beta Grooming and Marching Society

On every rung of the White House roost, each assistant ingratiates himself with the one above him. He doesn't care who knows it—for everybody's doing it. It's the rung that counts. He arrives early and stays late; flatters the wife; passes on gossip, acts as a bag man, arranges a leak, or ghost-authors an idea. It is not unlike the frenzied activity of his forbears in the rain forest who wanted to get up in the world. With prehensile tails securely clasping the nearest branch, they paid homage to their superior by delousing him in a meticulous grooming operation.

Sometimes the assistants go through this ignominious ritual automatically, needed or not. This was the case with the in-house Camelot sociologist Daniel Patrick Moynihan (later ambassador to India) in his tearful valedictory to Nixon (his reactionary target in the 1960 campaign) under full-dress cabinet staging.

As disciplined as most high betas are, there are occasional ones near the top who develop false presidential pregnancies. Though no one can usurp the title of president, a power vacuum at the top doesn't go unfilled. Sherman Adams found Ike wanting and filled the void until the *vicuna* fall. From the Watergate testimony, there is no question that what seemed to be three tough quarterback types (Mitchell, Haldeman, and Ehrlichman) turned out to be nothing but (very) offensive lineman—more groomers than vacuum fillers. In retrospect, the vacuum was (and still is) both literal and figurative.

Just as frequently, aides who ordinarily speak for, interpret, or take over minor presidential proxies may sense a void when there is none. In this unbelievable self-delusion, they may foolishly test the highest rung when they know full well that once a beta, always a beta. It's a sure death-wish, for the rarefied alpha atmosphere at the top is not only toxic but deadly for a beta. Few of them chance it. Bill Moyers, like few others, openly gambled for the stakes of proxy pinnacle power, telling none other than the super id of LBJ what was best for it. He wound up no different than an irrespressible young chacma baboon who overreaches his genetic status, loses, and is relegated to limbo—meatless and mateless, a political castrate.

Alter Egos, Zombies, and Cop-outs

On the other hand, betas like Ted Sorensen, who trust their instincts more than their egos, have no illusions. His niche was as JFK's alter ego and he well knew he would be comfortable neither below nor above his high beta status. Like Colonel House with President Wilson or Harry Hopkins with Roosevelt, he did as his programming bid and was happy on the perch he'd reached.

There are also in each administration closetsful of living zombies frequenting the old mansion. They are the ones banished from the West Wing because number 1 can't stand the sight of them, but who are still considered useful. Poltergeists like Arthur Schlesinger, Jr. and Richard Goodwin in the Kennedy regime, and the politically valuable leftovers Stewart Udall and Willard Wirtz in the Johnson era, were accorded only *vice presidential* pecking position by the top betas.

Then there are those whose genetic drive could neither tolerate dominance nor risk the gamble to take over. (New queen bees born into a hive soon realize there is no room at the very top and with no fanfare take off with a small select constituency to start a new colony.) Jack Valenti and George Reedy, two who never had it so good as in Johnson's White House, soon tired of low beta roles in the big fish bowl and opted to become big fish in more lucred bowls. The other types of genetic misfits were Packard (secretary of defense) and George Romney —chiefs in their own right at one time who couldn't tolerate for long droppings from the highest rungs and resolved their dilemma by staking out on the top of lesser heaps.

Declines and Falls

The psychological instinct for upward mobility isn't limited to individuals. There is also the constantly competing collective hierarchy of groups and agencies vying for position. The White House is always securely on top (except during Teapot Dome or Watergate scandals). The Departments of State, HEW, HUD, Commerce, etc., battle for favor and succeed or fail, depending on their leadership. For instance, the Department of State has always been very high on the roost, but when John Connally took over Treasury during a monetary crisis in 1971, Treasury was in and State was out. Now in 1974, with Kissinger as Secretary, State is in again.

But pecking orders, wherever they are, aren't forever. Genetic energy, like all else, declines with age and fatigue. As Konrad Lorenz has shown, a weakening leader in a flock of jackdaws doesn't last long but dies hard. An old buck in a herd of deer makes a greater and greater display of dominance as his prestige wanes. He desperately holds onto power against all comers. However, a constituency will sense a loss of power in an aging leader and be on the lookout for a replacement. Loyalty begins at home—it's *their* survival, not his, they worry about. Drawn and beleaguered, Nixon became arroganter and arroganter as Watergate sapped his vitality and staff. But he's bulled it through, even when he had to place want ads for office clerks and take barrel scrapings for cabinet secretaries. In the political lexicon, pride is absent, even in the old warrior. If you have to take your lumps, take them, but never give up until the last precinct is in.

The politician's end is a graceless thing, for his ego admits no defeat, even after the votes are counted. He goes back to the darkened political arena like an aging clown returning to the rung of his triumphs. He *Claghorns* his way onto the "floor" as if nothing had happened, greeting his old (and embarrassed) colleagues with in-house jokes, slipping in a little advice, winking and chuckling, momentarily reliving his salad days. Frequently he returns to hang around the fringes, in symbiosis, as a lobbyist or a "consultant"—to wheedle and flatter as he was once wheedled and flattered.

And so it goes on every rung of the political and governmental roost, in the campaign or in the bureaucracy, from the precincts to the presidency. Each rung produces its own cock of the walk. Each level biologically propagates itself, with only enough genetic momentum to reach its rightful place. They can talk about black power, woman power, and Polish power—but, all in all, the only power that counts is peck power. All power to the pecker (and you can say that again). There's nothing like sitting on top and as every chicken knows, the lower on the roost—the more mud in your eye.

VII

The Good Turf

(A Political Imperative)

> The territorial instinct may be fulfilled in many ways or simply for reasons of seizing. Man will fulfill his territorial instinct, as has been demonstrated, whether or not benefit will accrue.
>
> —Robert Ardrey

> The urge to control property and dominate one's peers in man is also an ancient biological trait that exists in the different form of territoriality and dominance among most, if not all, animal societies.
>
> —René Dubos

One of the most remarkable intellectual feats of the beetle-browed primitive politician was diverting the most peaceful animal instinct handed down to him into a sure-fire means of mass suicide. One of early man's first acts upon acquiring his new brain was to transform the territorial imperative, the best longevity insurance he ever had, into the deadliest game on earth. The old survival instincts, perfect for most mammals, were just not good enough for the thinking man.

His Brother's Reaper

It must be admitted, however, that though killing for land became a way of life (and still is), it was at first a necessity. The ancestor of *Homo sapiens* had no alternative but to hunt his protein rather than pick it off a tree when his green, leafy paradise was iced over or withered away by global cataclysms. But he could also boast of another first—he wasn't choosy about who the protein was, even his own brother.

71

This was purely human as Nobel Laureate Tinbergen explains it, it wasn't instinctive but second nature—part of man's character. This innovation must have put the fear of God into his simian brethren (intraspecies killing was unheard of before in animal history), but startling or not, it beat chasing rabbits and antelopes all over the landscape or glacier. Though these beasts were much more suited to his palate, on lazy days especially, it was much easier to simply knock his unsuspecting fellow human on the head and eat him. He also found that there was a bonus in it—he got his less fortunate victim's land and all that went with it—kith, kin, and kaboodle.

Early man can't be totally condemned for this; he was preoccupied with surviving, and at best it was catch as catch can. It was not surprising either (although it was a far cry from the behavior of his animal ancestors) that even after survival was assured and his tastes became more refined (lamb chops are not only tastier, but much less stringy than a tough human sirloin), he still wouldn't rid himself of the urge for brotherly blood—not so much for the blood as what came with it. He soon found that by being his brother's reaper, he might have lost a sibling but he gained a territory. And territory, he found, also meant power: He could move about easier, eat better, get more attention, more women, be healthier, live longer, and have a better time altogether. So early man, by a fortuitous ethical blind spot and a strong pull to the good life, found that doing in his fellows was a means to a comfortable and rewarding end—and he grabbed it.

Planned Errant-hood

Not all men were capable of dreaming up this enlightened way of life. The follower was—and still is—more or less content with what he already had. It was the facile political intellect that fashioned his supersophisticated solution to social life and abandoned the less violent territorial imperative of his animal ancestors (which used primarily bluff and bluster, rather than mayhem and murder).

Of course, if one wished to tie a more noble if teleologic

motive to the land hunger of the early politician, it could have been a subconscious means of population control, which all species must occasionally resort to. If so, the early politician had figured out the solution to the future population dilemma way before Malthus. To put it in doublespeak: contraction by expansion. And why not? That same brain invented fire, used tools, and developed language—why couldn't it have conceived a sort of planned parenthood? If this was the reason, it was a nervy gambit to deliberately limit his own growth rather than leave it to another species.

He made it a sort of intramural sport within his own species alone, rather than the willy-willy shark-and-sardine method of his predecessors (he even neatly legitimatized it later by the Geneva Convention, articles of war, and other niceties that made it more gentlemanly and fair).

Mind Over Manners

Of course, the primitive animal in its unsophistication was safer and more secure since each instinctually respected all others' territory. The unwritten etiquette of the wild was simply an ingrained politeness. Though modern politicians have a certain disdain for etiquette (an effete social custom equated with English teatime and striped-pantsed diplomats), it is the secret of success of the animal territorial imperative, whether in a cave or a nest. The ravenous lion or the tough, aggressive baboon instinctively slows down as he approaches his neighbor's boundary. Even the stag driven by deep hormonal rutting urges courteously detours around his next-door deer's territory.

The excitement of confrontation and deadly conflict is avoided in the animal world, and at best only a sham anger—a bluff—is enough to change an aggressor's mind. Robert Frost notwithstanding, it was not good fences that made good neighbors; no barbed-wire or chain-link fences or Maginot Lines were necessary. But these unsophisticated terms were too simple for the new human politician, who must do things his own way.

Every animal from asp to zebra, arthropod to primate, does it the safe and easy way: He may look, salivate, pant, and

desire, but he may not touch, grab, invade, or even liberate
his neighbor's property. But not political man. The simple
animal behavior pattern—that need for a haven of one's own
that was a sure-fire means of law and order—was rejected hands
down by human political leaders. First of all, it was too non-
competitive. What fun was it to wake up every morning with
the same old faces to lord it over? Second, the excitement of
new lands, travel, adventure, was man's way. And last, what
better way to show who's superior than by how much one has?
The new rational brain in the apelike skull just couldn't live
by the limited old-fashioned instinct of the lesser breeds. The
human politician did it his way: more Swiftian than Swift's
"modest proposal."

So what was good for three billion years for his ancestors
was not good enough for *Homo habilis*, not only the first so-
called human on earth, but the first arrogant animal ever.
Whether with mousetraps or computers, he has always been
bedeviled by an improvement mania; in his conceit, he had to
improve on the life-saving territorial instinct even if it killed him.

The Empire Builders

The hundreds of crushed human skulls of the Peking man
found at Choukoutien (one of man's anthropologic Edens) give
embarrassing evidence that our caveman ancestors went to any
extreme to expand—even (as we stated) to eating their own (an
unusual ethologic if not political happening). So our present-day
politicians come by their acquisitive traits honestly, if not peace-
ably, and use land as a means to show their competitive spirit,
if not their good sense. What super-salesman could have per-
suaded political thinkers like Napoleon, Bismarck, Teddy Roosevelt, or any presidential candidate that the old animal instinct
"to have and hold" was better and safer than their need "to have
and have more?" Our brainy political ancestors even convinced
their constituents into vying, fighting, and dying for empires
—on the battlefield or in the precincts (though the man in
the street is belatedly beginning to wonder who dies most,
for whom, and why).

The inherited enlargement complex is as prevalent in a Hottentot politician as in a member of Parliament. The grand obsession has been carried along from the time early man first pyramided his cave and savannah conglomerate; through that real estate emperor, the marauding Genghis Khan, adding steppe after steppe to his holdings; to the final drive for world *Lebensraum* by Adolf Hitler. It hasn't been bloodless, but anything goes in the pursuit of peace—and land.

This relatively new political instinct (about two million years old) is no less prevalent in a fledgling city councilman than in Alexander the Great. The beginner develops instant political diplopia—that is, one eye firmly fixed on the district recently won, the other roving for the next larger territory—as soon as he is sworn in. On election night, the contemplative look in the eye of the winning congressman reflects neither cerebration nor appreciation, just the silent planning of the next campaign for governor or senator. As the biography of the simplest and apparently least aggressive of presidential candidates, George McGovern, reveals, "His first political job, and each thereafter, was for the express purpose of enlarging his political platform, widening his audience and expanding his influence."

Our Daley Bread

In a territorial (or any other political) sense, we must again return to the compleat politician, the Honorable Richard Daley: mayor of Chicago, boss of Cook County, and master of all he purveys (a world in itself).

This plethoric eggplant-contoured (and colored) Southside Irishman has controlled a domain for twenty years as no jungle monarch ever controlled his. He exhibits first the most peaceful trait of the animal territorial instinct: defense against all comers. He keeps his boundaries as inviolate as the king of beasts, who daily anoints his outposts with his urinary spray as a gentle reminder to "keep off." The good mayor is as alert as any bull elephant scenting danger to those boundaries. His instinct protects the most genetically compatible herd of followers on the American political veldt by means somewhat less civilized than animal bluff. Rampant on the floor of the Chicago Convention in 1968, tusks raised, drawing his finger across his throat, he trumpeted his defiance in defense of his territory and tribe. He was as suspicious and xenophobic as any rhino when Abbie Hoffman and Jerry Rubin intruded on his Grant Park domain.

Such "peaceful" animal defense of what he already had in no way precluded his human political penchant for reaching for more. He ranged far beyond his jurisdiction and nominated and elected judges, governors, and senators. Armed with well-disciplined (and well-rewarded) delegates, whom he could count on to deliver, he got his piece of the U.S. and A. by crowning Jack Kennedy in 1960 (it would have been Nixon without Cook County), stood firm on LBJ in 1964, and in a fit of pique helped ruin Hubert Humphrey in 1968. He has been called on by Congress to intercede with presidents (both Democratic and Republican) and has been importuned by presidents to influence the Congress.

Like many another old buck knowing his time is near, he holds on with fierce pride and sagacious maneuvering. The blow to his pride dealt by the 1972 convention in Miami—from which neither George McGovern nor the Democratic party could have hoped to profit—was graciously (if gleefully) written off in the Nixon landslide, with Illinois a blatant accessory to the crime.

What held true for Richard Daley as he enlarged and secured his territory is no less true for ward leaders and presidents. Even at the very top, though chiefs of state try to suppress their subconscious urge for more, little gambits like Czechoslovakia, Poland, and Tibet help keep their hand in.

The politicians lower on the scale are more direct and open. They need no grandiose territorial excuses of "balance of power," or geopolitics, or the noble clichés of "making the world safe for democracy" and "wars of liberation." "Theirs is not to reason why, theirs is but to cut the pie," and they admit it. The only thing an Essex County (N.J.) boss remembers of "One World" is Wendell Willkie and one other politician who tried it another way and wound up committing suicide in his own bunker.

The Political Abacus

In the world of politics where more is better, what easier way to prove the winner and show strength than territory? Certainly, character, integrity, nobility, compassion, or any of those old values is no political yardstick—they're hard to exhibit and even harder to come by. But territory can be measured in front feet, acres, voters, districts, or even in square miles. The proof of the political clout is in the real estate. A freshman congressman or a county councilman shows his superiority only by the size of the district he controls—a senator even more, a governor more than that. (Who knows the name of the governor of tiny Rhode Island or sparse Nevada? Who doesn't know Rockefeller of New York or Reagan of California?)

Then of course, there's the president, who has just about as much land as he can legally get without the U.N. interceding—so what can he prove? The only territorial gambit he has left is to prevent others from getting more than he has (which is yet another excuse for trying for even more).

The Seedy Politician and the Glue That Binds

Up until about forty thousand years ago, the early nomad politician grabbed territory but it seemed to be getting him nowhere. He knew something was missing but couldn't put his finger on it. Here he was, generously spreading his seed all over the landscape, and what did he get for it? A polyglot mass of strangers he didn't even recognize, much less be able to organize his next time around.

The wanderer soon bowed to the inevitable and settled "down on the farm" (a cinch compared to hunting buffalo or depending on his aim with a rock or a spear for his dinner). Everything then fell into place. Though he had no great biologic insight and it was 39,900 years before Mendel, he soon caught up. The less he traveled, the more he reproduced only with those with whom he lived, worked, and played. The same seed began turning out its own replicas in looks, temperament, and intelligence (a gene pool it is called now); thus the origins of Irish or Italian, black or white, Mohammedan or Christian, and eventually Democrat or Republican. In other words, pools of sameness that stuck together naturally.

Power politics then really came into its own. It was a political dream. What a breeze to organize: nothing strange, nothing to fear, all one big happy gene pool with the same habits and goals, and territory to boot—all made to order for the political boss. The mixed genes of the fierce roving Hun left behind him the stolid German burgher, a world power (and menace) in every generation; the traveling Bedouin gave up his camel for an irrigated plot and built the glory that was Cleopatra's, even vying with mighty Rome for power and land. (On the other hand, the gypsies, who were never territorial-minded, are still a ragtag mass of no political significance.)

So as it went, the once happy-go-lucky bands turned into cadres of less happy, but more secure, followers—the rank and file of the party faithful, a breed that could be glued together. Born in territory and bound by biology, this one-of-a-kind pool soon learned to stuff envelopes, canvas neighborhoods, and man telephone banks. Strangely enough, they rarely come unglued.

Hate Thy Neighbor

As the follower was attracted by sameness, he was repelled by strangeness. Another old inborn trait, xenophobia, reared its ugly head. In an ant hill, burrow, or precinct, the suspicion of strangers is a psychological part of the territorial imperative that the politician not only loves but uses. The cry of "carpet-bagger" heard on the hustings makes a territory safe for incumbency. It destroys even a well known candidate gerrymanded from an adjacent district. It ruined the well-known Kennedy fringer from Nebraska, Ted Sorensen, in his two attempts in New York. (Bobby Kennedy was a special case.) An old political (and military) axiom dating back to a rat protecting its nest says it's easier to defend your own than attack a stranger's.

Party xenophobia proved newly Democratic John Lindsay's undoing on the national scene, and John Connally's turnabout will get him nowhere with Republicans. Even Middle America shied away from the strangeness of the intellect and wit of

Adlai Stevenson in 1952 and 1956, as it did from the black mayor of Los Angeles his first time around. Angela Davis must be the xenophobic pushover of all time as a quadruple minority: female, black, Communist, and intelligent.

The stomach of the leadership gene is only as large as its wide-lensed vision. Those with genetic sight as far as the eye can see will wind up president, prime minister, or dictator. Those who can see only as far as their own backyard settle down right where their territorial myopia keeps them, in their own backyard. It might appear that these nearsighted ones are throwbacks manifesting the good political manners of the animal in politely deferring to the territory of others. But it's often less respect and good manners than being scared to death of the wrath of an incumbent like Wilbur Mills or Carl Albert.

Every smart young baboon on the rise knows better. Biding his time, he waits for signs of senility or weakness, when his quarry is ripe. But occasionally the genes can't wait and the lure of territory is too much to resist. Anything can happen to the impatient ones, and usually does.

The Terra Firma Females

If the politician is an acreage lover, the females in his life love that good earth no less. They're magnetized by *terra firma*, as if every political district were a mother lode of uranium. A politician should never ask whether it's love or land—him or his turf. For pride's sake, the answer is better left unsaid.

The female has been attracted to male power and status from way back. Would young and beautiful females be drawn to the likes of either Strom Thurmond by his good looks, or to tiny, wizened (and powerful) Carl Albert for his physique and virility? On the other hand, there are few if any masculine takers, old or young, beating a path to the power of the de-maled Indira or Golda. A female robin would not give the time of day to a male until he has clear title to his own little acre. Rarely will an animal species fight and bicker over a female, it's always over the territory she loves so well. The uncommon nonaggressive male, whether hyena or chimpanzee, who can't stake out some bit of ground for his own will not only rave to depend on the leavings of the propertied class, but will also be hopelessly mateless. In the scheme of evolutionary things, a bird or beast not good enough to hack out a piece of land for himself just isn't fit to be a father.

So the Washington, D.C., Sacramento, Harrisburg, and Trenton ladies who follow power and property are not unusual phenomena, for though they follow closely in the footsteps of the robin, they behave even more like their closer cousin, the pinch-faced gibbon. This gibbon girl (like most other primates) is not satisfied with any run-of-the-mill male; she's on the make only for those with property and status. It's a rule she rarely, if ever, breaks. She may, on occasion, have a thoughtless fling with a young roué, but only those with holdings are allowed her "heated" charms—on a long-term basis.

If the average politician deludes himself about his inordinate attraction for, or luck with, superior or beautiful women, he soon realizes the limits of his sexual magnetism when the voters deprive him of his bailiwick and his bedmate in one fell swoop. Even the most eligible bachelor in congress John Brademus of Indiana is probably due a rude awakening (and a blow to the ego) when he finds most of his undying loves as evanescent as his power.

The real estate greed is no doubt born in the female blood —a primitive urge promising more security than happiness. For even after marriage, territoriality under the cherry blossoms hasn't helped the marital bliss of those male and female ground gainers. The high officeholder in his Potomac rancher or L'Enfant Plaza redoubt is just about as monogamous as the average leader of a wolf pack in his lair. One of the most obvious laws of politico-sexual dynamics is that the more territory a politician controls, the less influence and rapport he has in his own home.

Private Lives

The special mania of politicians for more and more somehow doesn't spill over into their private lives. Their personal territorial habits are less lethal, more like the animal's. It's quality rather than quantity they're after. To the politician, the world owes him his comforts and never let it be said that he ever paid for anything he didn't absolutely have to. As CREEP showed —at campaign time when money is no object, King Farouk would look like Scrooge by comparison.

The gorilla may not have an oval room or a wood-burning fireplace in July (like RMN) but he expects the special favors, privacy, and the best nesting area for his personal use. As the chief baboon has his hooting advance guard, heralding his approach in the routes and accesses to his territory, the politician expects his smooth-tongued advance man or screaming sirens and flashing lights to precede him. Just as the wolf pack waits till its chief has taken his choice spot in the den, the politician expects first-class jet travel, ringside seats, and hotel and restaurant reservations on demand as his constituents wait their turn or are turned away.

The Loved Ones

In death itself, the politician gives up his most precious possession with reluctance. Even as the last hymn is sung, as if clasped in rigor mortis, he yields, his hard-fought gains only to his wife, son, or daughter. They inherit this legacy, as surely as if it were written in his will. Robert Taft, Jr., of Ohio, Margaret Chase Smith of Maine, Adlai Stevenson III of Illinois, "Lindy" Boggs of Louisiana, Harry Byrd of Virginia, and Russell Long of Louisiana are among the many who naturally assumed control of the public territory of their deceased by divine right.

Then there are the Symingtons, the Bob Wagners, the Pat Browns, the Goldwaters, who allow a tithe of their political holdings to their progeny (but only a tithe) while still alive, to either wet their feet for the coming or to prevent political disinheritance tax. And why not? Whose genes, political personality, and ideology could be closer, and who could be more trusted to guard the faithful followers' territorial rights?

Frequently, the power is inherited with all the trappings of a monarchy. Like a blooded succession, vows are sworn, eulogies sounded, and festivities abound. The portrait of the deceased is prominently displayed as it would have been in the castle's great hall. The last resting place is visited annually in all solemnity and recorded photographically in living color. The name of the deceased is prayerfully invoked on proper political occasions, eliciting reverence and tears for the loved one and sympathy and votes for the legatee. The political estates of the Kennedys were not left to deteriorate; the mystique was nurtured, complete with an eternal flame at Arlington National Cemetery, for the remaining next of kin.

As death is no bar to passing on the territorial legacy, neither are prison bars a deterrent to holding it. True alphas, like former Mayor Curley of Boston, tenaciously hold onto their real estate even when in jail. The loyal subjects that come with the holdings keep the faith.

His Home His Castle

The follower is different. He is more like his howling monkey cousin, shrieking "This is my turf, my home is my castle." The political leader doesn't understand this limited state of mind and frequently has to waste valuable time and energy educating these dullards to the high life and excitement of expansion. He has to routinely soften and marinate these constituents like pieces of tough flank steak, convincing them that their nest is in danger to ready them for a little acquisition action. As Senator Vandenberg warned about the Truman Doctrine in 1946, "If Truman wants it, he'll have to scare hell out of the people first." That's what Teddy Roosevelt, Woodrow Wilson, FDR, and Truman did so well in their wars and what LBJ and JFK didn't do in theirs. Lately, the prosaic (and peaceful) follower instinct has been further fortified by the word getting around that more politicians than followers die peacefully in bed—their own.

No political system or social contract yet tried can beat the instinct of owning. As expected, the mind-expander communes of the sixties went up in hashish smoke as the common pad went down the drain. All of the love and brotherhood of the counterculture evaporated as the sophisticated Berkeley-type peace advocates battled ferociously among themselves for something of their own—just like the prairie dog or the herring gull. That was ten years ago. They are all now well ensconced in their own little vine-covered ranchers, dutifully paying their forty-year mortgage at 10 percent.

Even the Soviet peasant, religiously dedicated to Stalin, Mother Russia, and the collective earth, drudgingly plants and harvests his assigned quota on the collective (no more, no less), but energetically produces ten times as much on the tiny patch assigned him as a generous Soviet sop to the territorial imperative.

At a higher level in the Soviet establishment, the respected Lenin Prize winners and production czars would more readily part with their titles and medals than their own little *dacha* in the country.

To the human politician all property is fair game. His unique, insatiable territorial instinct, so different from that of his ancestors, shows him in every way the "Savage Noble," sitting on evolution's highest throne.

But it seems he's a goner, for he is playing a game with a stacked deck—against him. If he reverts back to the old animal territorial imperative, it's back to the rain forest, which in his present flabby state would be *finis*. If he continues the way he's going—in this Nuclear Age—the world must wind up as one great burned-out spaceship, the great Cinder-ella.

VIII

Sexual Capitolism

(Woman's Place is in the House, the Senate, or . . .)

> Women in politics commonly have masculine faces, figures and manners. In transplanting brains to an alien soil, God leaves a little of the original earth clinging to the roots.
>
> —AMBROSE BIERCE
> *The Devil's Dictionary*

It might be said that if God had wanted women to be politicians, he would have made them with thicker skins, grosser tastes, an unparalleled egomania, and the inclination and capacity to absorb a fifth of Old Forester in any one tough campaign day without the benefit of Lydia Pinkham's Compound.

Whether by cosmic design or chance, in the three billion years of animal history, only a handful of the million or so species (the South African phalarope and the striped hyena among others) are dominated by the female. If our present-day human phalaropophiles think they can buck this formidable fact and change their own natural endowments by edict, confrontation, petition, or constitutional amendment, they are smoking testosterone-cut hashish and bulling it through just like any male would flat on his back at the count of nine.

From the moment the sperm carrying the XX female chromosomes penetrates the ovum, the resultant female and all she can ever be has an uphill battle to be lord of the manor, much less break into the great game of politics. And just as surely, the male XY chromosomes make it natural for him to ply the hustings. Only an act of God or an X-ray machine can change this.

Notwithstanding all this fundamental biologic (or theologic) fact, every half-century (as is their cyclic nature), from Lysistrata and the Greeks down through Elizabeth Cady Stanton's followers, the suffragettes in 1919, to the most recent Friedan, Greer, Steinem liberationist surge in 1969, the weaker sex go on a well-deserved power-seeking binge. These hardy souls know full well the odds against flying in the face of evolution, genetics, their hormones (raging or otherwise), and the added indignity of male chauvinism. But they have to get it out of their systems. It's like a recurrent alcoholic's drying-out period, a compulsive cleansing of the soul.

Ms. the Ramparts

The feminist will insist in all seriousness that this time "it's it" and "our time has come." The lady gurus of the movement will Ms. the ramparts, whip up the cadres, cite John Stewart Mill and Millett, point proudly to Abzug, Chisholm, and Golda Meir, and drag that exploited bed-making housewife, curlers and all, away from her color TV and *As the World Turns* to march three miles down Fifth Avenue on a bone-chilling March day carrying a sign heavier than a garbage pail and two vacuum cleaners.

All of this hardly occasions the shrug of an old-line political shoulder. The pro knows all the symptoms of these semicentennial *female troubles*, not too different from the recurrent political acne of the campus kiddies. Both are annoying, but as benign as the common cold. He also knows it takes only a bottle or two of aspirin and forced fluids (preferably gin) to ride it out. As a dyed-in-the-wool historian of these movements, the old pol can cite chapter and verse of the rise and fall of these amateur hours.

With the proper timing, the pol tosses them the proverbial political bone, like suffrage in 1920 and a female cabinet member ("Ma" Perkins) in 1933. But unlike the cynical and suspicious male, these aspiring female political leaders (other than those few elected) grab the bone, and the promises of more to come, in good faith. In 1972, Larry O'Brien played the scene like a Hamlet, intoning in his sepulchral bass baritone that he "couldn't agree more with them." Then with much fanfare and press hoopla he appointed a co-chairperson, who sat uncomfortably for a few days at the convention with a gavel she couldn't lift (in the odd hours) then was happy to disappear like a wraith as, unmindful of her presence and without a hitch in stride, the males got on with the *real* business of politics.

The Obscene Gene

If history repeats itself, the political pro will pay no more heed to these distaff sorties than he does to any other reform flurry. Conceding a well-deserved point or two for appearance's sake, he has no notion of letting them spoil either his fun, his games, or his livelihood.

But whether it's male chauvinistic indifference and repression or just a natural genetic passiveness in the female that allows male politicians to get away with their patronizing ways and dominance, the militants put on their blinkers and see it as conditioning only.

> The gene is obscene and
> Pavlov's their love
> It's nurture not nature
> Enslaving their creature.

They give genetics the back of their hands, for it they didn't, they'd have no gam to stand on. They can't be faulted for this maneuver. It's easier to make the male pig the fall guy than God or evolution.

As the Lib litany goes, the intellect of the male and female is born equal, so why shouldn't the female also be a politician? Even if it were true, which it isn't (the male and female brains are born as different as Richard Nixon's from Frederick Chopin's), what in the world do brains have to do with politics? But as it is we know that the political part of the convolutions, gray matter, and frontal lobes has had a disuse atrophy since its very inception and is only of limited use, even to the male, so what kind of argument is that?

Politics is an instinctual game, and in our evolutionary history, it has been as male as football or war. The male animal was the politician way before the human brain made the scene. From our earliest history as a mammalian rodent, it was the male tree shrew—the male only—who led the female of the species from her humble beginnings through the dismal swamps all the way to the ladies' auxiliary and fund-raising theater parties. And as we progressed, gene by gene up the ladder, those leadership nerve pathways in the male brain were grooved in a political way, just as the female brain was set in less unattractive but possibly more productive ways. Both sexes had to play their own special, if different, roles for survival, they did and they will. If conditioning had little to do with it up until the human evolved —why now?

Virility or Fertility—That is the Question

In the male-eat-female scheme of things, because the male had the hormone that made him bigger and stronger, it was only natural that he was the one to defend the nest. If he had to reproduce too, he certainly couldn't defeat anything, at least not in the last trimester of pregnancy, during labor, or in the first six months after. If he had to both defend and reproduce, it wouldn't be long before only the sterile males, unencumbered by pregnancy and suckling, would dominate by force. But if those sterile ones took over and then couldn't reproduce themselves (especially as leaders), it would go against the very grain of nature and the leadership subspecies would die out. Evolution works in wonderous ways. So the male was spared her chore, and the female was spared his.

If this were not so, imagine the pregnant situation of any of our four-legged ancestors, belly dragging the ground, beating back the fangs of a lean, hungry predator attacking the nest. How could the early male have the stomach (no pun intended) to forage for food in a constant state of morning sickness? Or again, how could he have gone out to conquer the world with a litter of little ones swinging from his teats and others underfoot whining for a Good Humor pine cone?

The militant ladies who want their sisters to shoulder a gun and dig in the mines won't admit to the research of even their own distinguished ethologist, Jane Lancaster—"biology places role restrictions on women."

Fitness for roles is no less important in the political than in the evolutionary arena. Could Congresswoman Patsy Mink, as tough as the skin of Hawaiian pineapple and even more deadly serious, pun, parry, or push over the giant bibulous "Tip" O'Neill—her Democratic whip—if her hormones were raging. Or could pink, plump, and powdered Bostonian Louise Day Hicks, if she were subject to hot flashes and depressions, finagle an appropriation bill out of Wilbur Mills' Ways and Means Committee? Could one keep a straight face with Bella Abzug bellying up to McCloskey, the tall, lean crew-cut congressman from California, if she had a foot of uterus intervening?

No one's to blame. It all started with Eve. She should have known better than to let Adam take a bite of that apple. He's used it on her ever since. In his male lust, he immediately got her into trouble and made her the sexual fall person. After he'd worn her down to a nubbin with pregnancy and what went with it (kids, housework, and cooking), he, fresh as a daisy and free as a bird, went out into the world to sharpen his political skills and learn to be king of the hill.

Up Against the Wall

Since that beginning, millions of years of natural selection (and a touch of chauvinism) have made the female even more adapted to the connubial home than to the political House, and it was no different in the PreCambrian mud than it is in the present campaign jungle. But instead of taking it as a badge of grace and honor to be relieved of the tedious, niggling harangues and petty back-biting of politics, the present feminists regard their lot as a mark of Cain.

Just because she is physically, mentally, and emotionally different (the latter two are rarely admitted) is no reason to believe that a male cabal is trying to pin the female to the kitchen wall. Is it necessarily shameful that she is geared better (as male scientists point out) to a peaceful, contemplative life (even with *Kinder, Kirche,* and *Kuchen*)? Would she be more proud to have been born to lead a half-mad existence of selling her soul in cutting a deal or boorishly plotting, conniving, wheeling and dealing, and leaning over a bar till the wee hours trading banalities? Being excluded would rather make her more human, if less political—which is what we all aspire to.

It only happened by chance, for as John Kennedy said, "Life is unfair." The male just couldn't help his plight. When early man came down from the trees, who else but he, with the muscle, could hunt? And though not the brighter of the sexes (which is proved every day by who really hustles for whom), his brain was sharpened in the ways of the hunt, along with his ability to kill a wolf at sixty paces with a rock. It was his dumb luck to have to compete with the tiger and mammoth. He had to either become the most wily, devious, characterless creature on earth—or dead. One or the other. (The female shouldn't complain of being spared these options.) It was the male, always on the run, who in the daily crunch had to use every trick his poor gray matter could conjure up (which is no great virtue) just to keep him alive. Knowing he couldn't catch an antelope by himself or outstalk or outfang a tiger, his only alternatives were to either organize a mob to outman and outwit these creatures in order to have a meal ticket, or become one. He did the obvious.

It was only he who had to do all of those political things. It was not the Zsa Zsa Gabors of the cave in their fancy skins who had to kill for their supper, work with a team, maneuver their neighbors, or plan to do them in. Even if the female had the killer instinct, she didn't much need it. Unless she was protecting her young against predators or her man from younger females, she was relatively unchallenged inside the cave and protected without. She was also relieved of the male's onerous duty of leading, ordering, and placating—decisions, decisions—just to feed and protect himself, and her, the producer. She only had to do for the reproduced, which is no mean job but no practice for politics. Nor did it stimulate her to explore new fields, originate tools and weapons, compromise and conspire.

Practice Makes Politics

So it was not by any special mental capacity that males became so politically brainy. How could they but help it with a million years of human and a billion years of animal practice? St. Thomas Aquinas said it loud and clear centuries ago, "government involves more art than ethics—in other words more practice than theory."

The political shrewdness of LBJ took eons of evolution. His particular ancestors whipped their powerful scaley tails in the sludge of the primeval Pedernales, frightening those other Texas predators. Further up the scale, they bared their canines in defending their pride, barked their orders, and maneuvered their packs to encircle and close in on a prey; and in their first step up to the heavenly preserve, they made love to the most moon-eyed, simian-lipped, silky-furred female to finally produce his domineering great-uncle a hundred times removed. This eventually brought forth a grandfather quick on the draw, who could outbargain a cattle dealer, string up a cattle rustler, talk his way out of jail, or organize a posse. Though this didn't take real thinking ability, it took an automatic kind of political mental agility, born in the blood.

The gentle female ancestors, though not putting their hides on the line had to think just as clearly for different reasons. Their job was not as glamorous or adventurous as the hunt, but it wasn't a carefree shopping spree or a Thursday afternoon Mah-Jongg game either. Keeping the fire going, searching for grubs, gathering berries, and, most important, using all their compassion, patience, empathy, and persuasiveness to control and condition their red-blooded Neanderthal offspring was a full-time job. It was only dangerous if she didn't please her spouse. In those days, the male's bark was all bite. If the larvae weren't prepared just right or the kids were lost when he got back to the cave, there was hell to pay. Just to survive her partner took some real psychologic doing on her part.

Stamp Out MCP Hormones

It's always been an enigma, if, as the feminists say, the female is what she is only by male conditioning, how the simple-minded male was smart enough to get out from under the maternal training (at least six years even in a chimpanzee), turn the tables, become a chauvinist, and then put his sister in bondage. The answer is to be found nowhere else than in that domineering political gene—born in the womb.

The female of each species had to become intuitive in handling children, in competing with other women, and in outsmarting and controlling the overmuscled male just to stay alive. It became her stock in trade, but it wasn't the same as outmaneuvering a pack of wolves or a strange tribe of half-man. It will take her a thousand generations of practice to catch the guilt in a shifting political eye, the sign of weakness by one wrong word, the fear in the quiver of a nostril, or the admission of double cross in an imperceptible movement of the hand. To the political pro, all this comes naturally. If this is true, what about the occasional female pro—how does she come by that instinct?

Every female has some male in her and every male a little female. Neither is all or none. But whether a female shaves or a male must wear a brassiere depends mainly on the relative strength of the male sex hormone that circulates in them. It's not the female hormone that makes the difference, it is the male one that affects the mind and the instincts as well as the body.

There are all gradations of masculinity, down to the small minority who couldn't lead a poker player to the refrigerator. And likewise, at the bottom of the feminine ladder, there is a small group of women in wolves' clothing who would have done as well as Teddy Roosevelt charging up San Juan Hill. There aren't too many of these chemically-toughened, competitive females around because they were either killed off by the early male for being uppity or were hormonally sterile and didn't reproduce their kind. Some of the androgenous ones did persist and reproduce in spite of their hormonal discrepancies. They are our present-day female politicians, and it is no wonder that they act the role.

Sick Gloria Intransigent

Besides the certain grooved-in male political mentality, there is the matter of emotions in politics. Any early man making his living on the dangerous savannahs who wasn't as cool as a cucumber, steady as an oak, and unflinching as a stalking lion was due to be buried like a turnip. It took a levelheaded nervous system, full of frosty synapses, to face a charging woolly mammoth. Those who panicked or sat down and cried, wound up "finger-licken good," never to reproduce their flappable kind. It took cool male political guts, passed all the way down to a Dick Daley. Kicked out of the 1972 Democratic Convention with only a shrug and a grimace, he didn't get mad, he got even. In 1968, when they slurred his machine on the "Stockyard" floor, he didn't get crying mad or foot-stomping mad, he got fighting mad—and again, he got even.

If we zoom back in on that 1972 convention in Miami, there sits the stone-faced Goddess of Liberation, Gloria Steinem (turned politician), on the floor racked by heaving hysterical sobs because the insignificant South Carolina resolution on abortion was killed. Or Bella Abzug, charging for McGovern's Gary Hart like a wounded rhinoceros, spewing four-letter words like unguided missles for the same trivial cause—and for all the world to see. Unlike Daley, their reactions did neither any good.

Then there is Congresswoman Shirley Chisholm always threatening to quit in a fit of pique because a House committee was frustrating a bill of hers (Congressman Otto Passman had taken a beating on foreign aid for twenty years before he got his way). Even Golda, always proudly pointed to as the dominant achiever of the Ms. generation, admits making decisions on the basis of emotion.

There's Nothing Like A Good Cry

But then, the female from way back had every right to let her primordial emotions go—and it wasn't a matter of life or death if she did. It's not easy to change those reflexes overnight. In fact, they are what saved her sanity. What else could she do but let out a primal scream to ease her tension when the kids brought a leopard home on a leash? With her connubial life as it was, she was always the scapegoat and had to have some outlet. If the fire went out, the kid was mauled by a bear, or she couldn't dig up enough grubs and berry delicacies to sate her lord and master's demanding palate, her only defense was a hysterical, crying, floor-beating jag. To top it all, why shouldn't she be allowed some small means of showing her anger by a shrill, clawing hassle at those tempting svelt, young, flossy-furred things that came flouncing through the ferns, unencumbered and un-ravaged by the vicissitudes of childbearing?

It took less a cool head than a kind and open heart for the female to survive that frustrating life. She came by her particular psyche and intellect just as the male came by his. And she has dutifully passed this temperament along to a degree in her XX chromosomes even to the woman account executive, the garden club president, and the elected officials of her sex.

The Nutcracker Sweets

This last group, the lady pol in or out of the role they play, are rarely the *Vogue* ad type. Take our three present-day women leaders of nations: Madame Bandaranaike of Ceylon, Indira Gandhi of India, and Golda Meir of Israel. First, there is not a feminist among them, which is not surprising. As Ms. Meir publically stated, "It's a lot of foolishness" (Prime Minister Ben-Gurion congratulated himself on having "a real man in the cabinet" when Golda was appointed). None of them is the epi-tome of the male ideal of the feminine face or figure nor could the doorman at St. Laurent's or Elizabeth Arden's be con-demned for casting a quizzical glance at these hard headed female politicians who apparently still believe in miracles. It would be improper and ungentlemanly to comment on the fact that though all three may have had ecstatic married lives while they lasted, all three of the ladies' husbands are dead and two of them were divorced before they died (and no takers since). (Neither will any allusion be made to the similar fate of the male preying mantis—or the Black Widow's ex.)

As females, they are no doubt all deeply devoted to peace, so it's probably just coincidental that one of them has just completed participation in her second war in six years (the last as chief of state), another has recently finished a highly satisfactory war of liberation, and the third has been on the verge of civil war twice. Notwithstanding this unfeminine behavior, it would be difficult to mark their level of femininity. The only true criterion is: Would you want your dear old grandpappy to marry one?

Speaking scientifically, give a woman enough testosterone and she'll climb Mount Everest and hang every MCP in sight; give a male enough estrogen, and he'll want to nurse a baby. If testosterone is injected into a female guppy or monkey, in three months she'll lead the school or troop. Though this gives us some idea of the hormonal influence on a political future, it does not prove that we can make a politician by the needle, but only emphasizes that by the grace of God and his testicular luck, the male is not ravaged by a cyclic nature.

She's Got Rhythm—The Period Piece

The male chauvinist has unfairly used the woman's monthly physiologic cycle as an example of the instability of her intellect and her emotions. Male-dominated Merrill Lynch, Pierce, Fenner, and Smith won't let most women trade on the commodity market because of it. But though the lone Soviet female cosmonaut admits she is fearful of guiding a spaceship during that special time, it certainly should not necessarily cripple a latent political talent, even if she had to spend eight days a month nursing symptoms of premenstrual tension, hair-trigger responses, killing headaches and cramps, and missing a few crucial votes. It would be evened out in the male time-wasting frailties with non-political cronies in a boozy haze or with excessively political young females in sexual debilitation.

Another of the most unfair, sneaky tricks of the male politician is denigrating and taking advantage of the female in politics, because in her declining years, she is subject to the ravages of menopause. He shrewdly watches for the telltale signs and swoops in during those hot flashes and cold sweats, pulling deals she wouldn't ordinarily be part of and conning her to vote for the most preposterous of his pet bills.

Dr. Saleem A. Shah of the National Institute of Mental Health has stated that the hormonal causes of abnormal behavior and violence in the female are as important as the psychologic or sociologic ones. Knowing the present state of abnormal political behavior, should the female politician be encouraged to add to this delinquency? Considering the national interest, it should give the voters pause.

Government Bonds—For Males Only

In either the male or the female, as in all of evolution, only those talents or instincts that were needed developed. And if there was one trait that could have given the female a political potential, it would have been the bonding syndrome described by social anthropologist Lionel Tiger. According to him, bonding occurs only in the male. It draws the young acned male to hang around the drugstore and poolroom and belong to the West Side Demolishers, and it likewise induces the adult Babbitt to join the Masons and the KKK and the male politician to while away a lifetime in bourbon camaraderie. It's part of the male psyche and has been so since he had to chase the deer and buffalo with other males to survive.

The male had to hunt or die; the female didn't. That same bond of teamwork and loyalty that allowed him to beat it out in the primordial jungle goes in spades for the political jungle. A campaign team, a convention strategy, passing a bill, working up a filibuster, or beating a cloture vote requires the bond. It can be predicted bonding may well save Richard Nixon's impeachment neck as it did President Andrew Johnson's conviction. That well-bonded male club, the Congress, will find the right excuses. Trading votes and bargaining on issues, pressuring, bribing, lobbying, jawboning, and arm-twisting have a solid basis in bond and the male hormone. This inherent male faith in one another and their inborn feel for their unwritten rules and guidelines can't be learned. And only the *male* politician thrives on it —in the barroom, the locker room, and the Senate cloakroom (where even his bourbon is bonded).

This is a frustrating deterrent to the aspiring female politician. She resents this natural obstacle and she should. Bella Abzug, as raunchy in speech as Joe Namath, as genteel as a Sumo wrestler, and as cagey as a Soviet wheat dealer, couldn't break the bond barrier with her skid row linguistics or her knee-to-groin tactics. Regardless of her feminine charm, she's about as welcome in a committee room as Ralph Nader is in the board room of General Motors. Even Helen Delich Bentley, the chairperson of the Federal Maritime Commission, a dozen-cigars-a-day lady, can't get her slipper in the door of the male political club.

This sticks in the craw of even those women not competing in the male jungle. There are more internecine battles, nagging, and going home to mother over those male bonding nights at poker and stag dinners, or over football, golf, or fishing widow-hoods, than over finding that telltale sign of "lipstick round the collar."

The lack of a bonding syndrome blew the Women's Caucus to bits before they got to the 1972 Democratic Convention. Goaded by Germaine Greer, Gloria Steinem and Betty Friedan (hardly on speaking terms) and politicos like Shirley Chisholm, Patsy Mink, and Bella Abzug (also not very friendly) were at each other's throats before the bell sounded for the first round (strangely enough none of them were in Gallup's most admired women's list). By midbout, the ring looked like Macy's base-ment during the January White Sale—Blacks, ethnics, elected officials, housewives, and volunteer types scratching and tearing for their share of whatever it was each wanted to the tune of Muzak's "Ride of the Valkyries." At the final bell, it was a draw by simultaneous technical knockouts.

There is great admiration and respect by many peace- (in-the-family) loving males for the Lib Movement and *Ms.* maga-zine, and empathy for, if not condoning of, the Equal Rights Amendment to the Constitution, but the lack of that age-old bonding instinct will always make the political nut tough to crack for the female. Unlike the male, kin is more important than kith to the female, and she has no qualms about following a male chauvinist. But the testosterone-knit voters stick together as if genetically welded and bound to vote for only their own.

It's a tough combination for the female politician to beat. If John Lindsay were to run against any female (Bella included) for any office with only females voting, Jimmy the Greek would put his money on the handsomest, if not the best, politician since Marcus Antonius. But it's the way it is, and *his-story*, not *her-story*, has etched the stone no differently for eons.

Fifty-Year Progress Report: Negative

Either the male politician knows his anthropology or he is a born social psychologist, else how could he have been so cock-sure that the Nineteenth (suffrage) Amendment wouldn't knock him out of the box? But here it is, over fifty years after, with 53 percent of the voting public female, yet there are no female governors nor major city mayors, only thirteen women in the Congress (there were eighteen in 1960 with two senators), and not a single female Senate or cabinet member. Some say this is the result of cultural male conditioning, and it may be, though the female has been a lot less conditioned since 1960 than before. Worldwide, even the least fair of the sex hold down fewer than 5 percent of the seats in the nations' parliaments. If, as they say, progress is being made, it doesn't show on an adding machine, or else it'll take another thousand years before they even pull up to the male—and patience is not one of their virtues.

If they aren't getting a fair shake from the Western male world, they should from the East—at least in Russia. For Lenin and Engels were two of the first patron saints of the feminist movement in the self-proclaimed most egalitarian nation on earth. So it couldn't be chauvinism (it's not legal in Russia) that prevents the talented female politician from gaining even a toehold in the Kremlin hierarchy. The Soviet trades and professions from street sweeper to physician are predominantly female (they even have a cosmonaut) so what keeps them off the Presidium? Why are there only 4 women out of 133 on the Central Committee and no first secretaries in any province or region, even though opportunity is guaranteed by law? With equal education and opportunity and no discrimination, what's left to blame it on but that dirty little gene?

The Hands That Rocks the Cradle . . .

As an uplifter of the spirit of the so-called drudging housewife, there is an old saw that goes "Behind every good man is a good woman." No doubt it's true, only it doesn't refer to the faithful spouse. Though much political credit is given Ladybird Johnson, LBJ would have made it had he been married to Janis Joplin. The Bird had little to do with the genes that the little old pipe-smoking lady on the Pedernales bequeathed him. And that political gene, with just a little bit of luck, is all that counts.

In a proxy sort of way, the hand that rocks the cradle does rule the world. The ladies may not themselves have the classic, if unattractive, traits to sit in the seat of power, but they have a lot to do with those who do. Not unlike a Spanish queen who transmits hemophilia to her young prince or like any mother who bequeaths color blindness to her male offspring, the female has the honorable role of carrying the political inheritance—to males only. But, as with any carrier, the traits may not show in her. She may appear as female and as apolitical as Marilyn Monroe, but political progeny do not occur without her input. (Frequently in primates, there is even a female political hierarchy whose progeny are guaranteed leadership, for they will only conceive with an alpha [leader] male.) To produce a dominant rat or a congressman, the proper mix must mate, male and female.

The Tell Tail

Because of the naturally demure and passive characteristics in the female tiger or human, it may be difficult to identify the political lady. Her demeanor usually obscures her real importance in political life, as with the gentle-appearing Rose Kennedy or a dainty baboon. However, there is one dead giveaway, one that glows like the Scarlet Letter. In the animal world, the one true test of a female political gene carrier is whether she goes for position, power, and territory. In crows or chimpanzees, this triad tails the female donkey. Those three lures are the baubles that attract that special female to mate with the best (if not the brightest) alpha she can lay her paws on. Though in human females there may be some shades of difference from their animal sisters, the Martha Mitchells, Marion Javits', and the hordes of young "Capitol Hill girls" (who rarely cavort, consort, or marry off the reservation) also reveal themselves by those self same tendencies. As the distinguished naturalist, Eliot Howard, described it, he never knew of a male bird with territory to lose a mate nor of a male bird without territory to gain one.

The political intuition of the alpha gene carrier can spot a winner four to eight years away, which may also account for how so many of these not so tender traps latch onto their prey early. It must be some inscrutable genetic attraction not yet scientifically discernible, for from what is observed, a genetically competent female doesn't need sexual come-ons—well hardly, if Eleanor, Bess, Mamie, or Pat are examples—nor does she have to compete with her tongue or her brains. One of the homeliest, gentlest, and quietest chimpanzees in Jane Goodall's forest observations was Flo, a great political producer.

Some females, though they appear to be potential political spouses and grasp at the treasure, for some obscure reason never make it. Barbarous Barbara Hower and salacious Sally Quinn, political dilettantes, may be attracted to power, live with it, sleep with it, talk and write about it, but, unlike Flo, could never nail the alpha coonskin to the wall. That old genetic magnetism just isn't there.

"Msculinity?" (sic)

Another phenomenon that bodes ill for female political aspirations is the Clare Boothe Luce syndrome. Here is an anomaly (Arsenic and Old Luce they called her during her peculiar poisoning episode as ambassador to Italy). Now in her seventies, a fading replica of her once beautiful and political self, she won't do what nature and the feminists expect of her. She is as svelt a package as any female politician that's ever graced the hustings and as power-bent as any Roosevelt or Kennedy (she has been elected, appointed, commissioned, and is as comfortable in a scroungy back room inhaling stale tobacco fumes as she is at a Newport house party). Yet for some genetic reason, she was attracted to *money* power rather than *political* power, and at that had only one offspring. She should have been a sure thing to produce female political likenesses if she'd only have cohabited for the survival of her species.

The discouraging thing is that there are dozens like her with little chance for expanding the production of the female politicians. Of the thirteen congresswomen, approximately two-thirds are married, averaging not quite one child apiece—less than half the national average. These thoroughbred mares only seem to cross with a male ass (the generic, not the metaphorical kind) to produce sparsely—and, from the record, generally politically-sterile mules.

A Bed of Roses or a Garden of Ragweed

The life of a political spouse is no bed of roses, especially in Washington. She pays dearly for her political acquisition. Living with a prima donna, a savior, and a seer rolled into one is not what it is cracked up to be and probably not worth the initial lure of status and real estate. Talk about bedroom communities —the political household is not even that, for the man in office rarely sleeps in his own bed. As we said, on his semiannual "evening at home," he is a caged lion.

The feminists talk about exploitation of the female, and they need look no further than the political wife—as housey and mousey as they come. If there were such a thing as equal pay for equal work, the government check should go to her, not to him, with a bonus for working a hardship post. She raises the children, hires and fires the help, does the shopping, cooks, entertains his colleagues and constituency, substitutes on the home hustings, and alone hits a minimum of three embassy, three fat cat, and three official cocktails a week. In campaign years, all the extradomestic chores treble. All in all, she'd probably be less exhausted than her pioneer sister who pulled the plow and weeded the bean patch. This happy little situation would make the divorce rate a cool 100 percent if the voters didn't frown on divorce almost as much as on their representative's being indicted on bribery or malfeasance charges.

Congressional wives are rarely open to controversy much less fun. Other than wives such as Marion Javits, who have the time and inclination for *haute couture* and *haute belle populi* of the Bill Blass and George Plimpton variety, they're much too busy working for their alpha. If there's going to be any fun and games in the family, he'll make up for both of them.

Political wives all voluntarily check in with Maxine Cheshire, Charlotte Curtis, and even *WWD*'s Candy Stroud, those talonded ladies of the Fourth Estate (to make sure of their fourth freedom), in self-defense, if nothing else. Wifely publicity is encouraged by the busy legislator, unless, of course, she gets more than he.

The sob sisters of the Betty Beale, Elizabeth Shelton, and Myra McPherson variety report on the other less exciting facts of Capitol punishment, such as Red Cross bandage rolling (yes, they still do it), the teas, and the political hen parties. But they dare not tackle the *lady* politicians of the Chisholm-Abzug breed. Even female politicians are for men only.

The De-Generation

It's a fact that the higher on the phylogenetic scale we go— and the larger the brain—the more time the big-brained infant is given at his mother's side to learn the ways of the world. The calf is weaned at six weeks, the horse at three months, and the chimpanzee keeps her young by her side for over six years. Not so the political kid in Washington. The political progeny might as well be cuckoo for all the by-the-knee education they get. As the cuckoo mother lays her eggs in somebody else's nest parental concern (like the political mother's) becomes anybody's problem but the cuckoo's.

The young capitol cuckoos are on their own before they feather. It's a wonder they learn the spoken language, much less normal behavior. It's to be supposed they learn from their peers, which is about as jungle-oriented as they can get. But luckily these lapses don't show up on the clean-cut family political portrait; if they did, it would be more like Dorian Gray than American gothic.

The kiddies, of course, are caught up in the glamor, publicity, and freedom from cloying adult interference. If nothing else, this keeps the Capitol police and juvenile courts busy straightening out and hushing up the consequences but as it's explained after each juvenile Kennedy or Shriver trial, pot, violence, and reckless driving is part of the growng up process for the young political lions.

But Could She Be President?

We've been *skirting* the real issue. A female may be physically, intellectually, or emotionally fit to be a politician—but could she be president? Shirley Chisholm faced up to this challenge, and in her first try at national primaries, did remarkably well. It was in no way a landslide but she did get a sprinkling of family and friends and with a little bit of luck she may have come even with Sam Yorty's primary vote. The electorate just has to get used to a campaign without bombast, fence sitting, demagoguery, and other male campaign ploys. It was only a starter, but she showed real male initiative in beating black Congressman Diggs, and the noisy Conyers, Julian Bond, Reverend Abernathy and a dozen others to the punch, running with the ball before the black caucus had finished its political soul breakfast.

But woman's turn will eventually come, for as the feminists have always insisted, only a "she" can lead us to a lasting peace through her natural sensitivity, her empathy, her compassion, and her abhorrence for violence. Only nit-picking chauvinists would point out that the suffrage cry fifty years ago was "give us the vote and we'll end all wars," since we've had thirty or forty in that period. And though Indira Gandhi did not imitate her passive, pacifist namesake in the Bangladesh massacre, nor was Golda Meir the oversolicitous, motherly, chicken-noodle-soup type with the Egyptian invaders or the Palestinian guerrillas, it could be worse—wait until a Barbara Walters heads a state.

Contrary to conventional wisdom, woman may be something special politically. She may not have to work her way up. If she did, she'd be at too big a disadvantage—there are too few to choose from, with no female governors or Senators (the usual source of male presidents). But with her superior (if special) talents, she may not be suited as well for the lowly precincts— only the presidency. After all, as Watergate has proved, it's character not charisma that counts in the highest office. The talents and traits that would hinder her in the political gutter may exactly fit her for the *haute monde* of politics. Her natural character, devoid of indecision, gossip, backbiting, jealousy, and flightiness, may far outweigh her hormonally-charged disabilities.

Baby Blue Bombers and Lunar Calendars

We can only guess how she would conduct herself in the highest office, but to whatever degree she has a gender role, conditioned or not, her feminine tendencies would surely color her presidency, just as a male's does his. Wouldn't Brezhnev cock one of those shaggy eyebrows in respect and admiration if that special Russian logic in the SALT talks came face to face with a woman's intuition? (Has the orthodox male logic had anything but token results at the UN so far?)

Could the well-bonded Congress put up with the fury of a female president scorned? Would George Meany buckle under to sexuality more easily than he did to LBJ's arm-twisting? Could she get *her way* with the Pentagon or change her mind after a Supreme Court decision? And maybe just as important to capital morale, would an astrologer replace Billy Graham on Sunday mornings and would needlepoint replace the Redskins on autumn Sunday afternoons? This is what we don't know.

But we have reason to believe that a woman in the White House might not keep as tight a fist on the budget, and when she feels low she might go out and buy herself a new bomber or indulge in a robin's-egg-blue battleship. In the process, she might overdraw her checking account—but, as always, she would make do. On the other hand, she wouldn't invite every international Tom, Dick, or Harry as house guests just because she met them on the way home from China or Russia, or because they had a good deal she couldn't refuse. Nor would she consider shopping for tanks and guns in April when they're 20 percent off in August. With the help problem as it is, "summer" White Houses on both coasts and at Camp David would definitely be out.

It's also inconceivable that a lady president would allow the price of gold to go out of sight with the tags at Tiffany's what they are; or would tax imports like Italian shoes or French fabrics; or let George Meany get away with those outrageous plumbers' wages; or allow the FDA to take wrinkle creams off the market.

After the Watergate experience, she would naturally keep her palace guard on its toes and run a tight ship. She would certainly not put up with the sloppy housekeeping at 1600 as revealed by the Ervin Committee—hanging the dirty linen out in the West Wing yard and splurging with the cookie-jar money. For obvious reasons, everything would run on a strict lunar calendar schedule. Secret tapings would definitely be out; eavesdropping and ouiji boards could be in. In a reverse double standard to compensate for those bitter years, all of the White House secretaries would be male or at least in between. The female cabinet would bow to sartorial decorum and dignity by refraining from wearing hair curlers at formal cabinet meetings. There would be no enemy lists, except for those Senate wives who questioned her choice of Givenchy over Blass at the last state dinner. The Security Council would not be allowed to rummage in the kitchen late at night, even with those flimsy national-crises excuses. The presidential yacht would not be referred to in the gender role of "she," and her personal aide would know that at the first sign of a hot flash, all radiators were to be inoperative (with cold chills, all radiators would be go).

Ready or Not

A female in the White House would no doubt be an unusual national experience for all of us. If the female were to reflect herself in office as we know her in her present status, it would not be dull—unless being on tenterhooks is a dull experience. The normal male reaction would predictably be the husbandlike far side of paranoia. Wall Street would tremble at the thought of the president's Council of Economic Advisors adding a clairvoyant and a necromancer to its team, and the State Department would dissolve in its own jelly as she changed its priorities from NATO, China, and Japan to India, Israel, and Ceylon.

From the record, it doesn't appear that there is any great

wave of national sentiment for a lady president, and there is even less cold evidence of political capability, but maybe in this era of sexual quotas, antidiscrimination, and equal opportunity, we should try it—ready or not.

So regardless of two million years of biologic precedence and the lack of female experience or even the desire to compete, organize, or dominate other women, plus the absence of a bonding syndrome and the presence of physiologic frailties—can anyone with even an iota of sound female logic come up with any rational objections why females shouldn't have their day in the political sun? Other than the problems of getting her elected, her political future seems unusually bright.

IX

The Preen Machine

(Take One Part Politician, Add . . .)

Politics, in a sense, has always been a con game . . . and as the American voter insists upon an illusion, the politician must embellish the illusion particularly if he wants to be president. . . .

On TV it matters less that a candidate does not have ideas. He need be neither statesman nor crusader—only show up on time.

—JOE McGINNESS
The Selling of the President

Politicians in their present semicivilized state have gradually suppressed their embarrassing instinct to howl, roar, and chest-thump their way to power. Though at campaign time there wells up an inevitable tendency to revert to type with a bit of the Huey Long/John Connally bellow-and-bombast, they are now above suffering that sort of undignified *advertisement for themselves.* In the grandeur of its newfound mature and human status, the cult of leadership could hardly afford to demean its image by crassly putting its own foot in the door like a Fuller Brush man. It is not only undignified and pushy, it hasn't worked of late.

Though the stentorian boom of a senatorial larynx could carry as far as a gorilla's on the political veldt, it could neither circumnavigate the high rises nor penetrate sprawling suburbia to reach the burgeoning numbers it takes to get elected. A surrogate (if not a more subtle) technique had to evolve—and it did. Now the alligator-shod candidate's foot is merely pressed to a pedal and a highly mechanized apparatus springs into action. It does the job in the manner and efficiency of everything else born of late-twentieth-century technology, and to boot, the candidate is not spattered by the grease and oil of its machinations.

The machine itself is a thing of beauty, created in a neonish mélange of taste reflecting modern sensitivity and aesthetics as symbolized by IBM, Woolworth's, McDonald's Hamburger, and beaver tails. It is custom built for the epoch-makers, who lounge back with a minimum of effort and personal exposure and allow this chrome-plated, jet-propelled, power-packaged artifice—rumbling with the thrust of highly specialized talent, meshed with Xerox, Telex, video, and radio—to carry them to victory. Using every stratagem from brainwashing to electric shock, candidates are presented at their very best (if not their very selves).

Communication or Excommunication

The politician either keeps up with the *Times* or goes down with the *Sun*. Like his tool-making predecessors in the caves, he has since struggled through the stone, iron, and brass-band stages. Now it's all different. To be elected, his body and soul must be transmuted into merchandise and transmogrified unto film, tape, and video cassette, and then peddled like Listerine. How else could his immortal self possibly be communicated to the vast anonymi now crowding his megalopoli? Surely it would be a mortal sin to allow latent political greatness (generously in the offing) to go unheralded simply because not enough hands could be pumped or babies bussed in a congressional district the size of some nations. Word-of-mouth around the cracker barrel and the *Independence* weekly's fire-spitting editorials may have nominated that old stemwinder William Jennings Bryan and won the presidency for Abe Lincoln, but today such folksy means couldn't elect a county clerk to the courthouse in Death Valley. Even a unique style, reliable intuition, mellifluous speeches, and bottomless energy—the stock in trade of every good politician—aren't enough today. From the first tool maker to this age of technology and science, the machine is the thing —whether with roadbuilders, dentists, or politicians.

Gilding the Lily

There is no question that the Preen Machine is efficient and leaves little (if anything) to chance, talent, or even the imagination. Only a political fool would do without one, but it does take its toll. Politics, once the mixed bubbly of competition, travel, sex, and power, is now more funereal than ethereal, more pall than play. The once irrepressible, fun-loving spirit and spontaneity of former Veep Alben Barkley, Mayor Jimmy Walker, or even FDR (and colorful Earl Long of Louisiana can't be passed over with the exotic stripper, Blaze Starr, in his campaign entourage) has been patiently recycled into an austere, unrecognizable milky plastic of indefinable character.

Imagine, just for starters, the process of gilding the political lily. This flower (about as delicate as a desert cactus) must be taken apart, petal by petal, and put back together again, a stranger to its own seed.

The pristine specimen is first slimmed down and youthened up, teeth are capped, hair tinted, and beard softened. Lights and makeup fill out the hollows, absorb perspiration, smooth the wrinkles, and firm up the jowls. In speakeasy surgery, eye bags are removed, dewlaps resected, and hair plugs (à la Proxmire and Thurmond) implanted. Heels are elevated for the stunted like Carl Albert and Charles Percy and their chairs are piled with cushions and their podia lowered. Gestures are practiced and speech is coached, voices are modulated to the statesmanlike tones of Senator Harold Hughes and sometimes even trained to the *basso profundo* of Everett Dirksen. Thoughtful phrases (written by talent the politician has never met) are read from a robot teleprompter that assures no hint of personality getting across. And forever lurking in the shadows are the trusted men of medicine or psychotherapists (like Nixon's *Dr. Hutschnecker*), ready to erase hangups, suppress fears, and bolster confidence.

To paraphrase Barry Goldwater, these cosmetized, psychologized, mechanical things are "less a choice than an echo." But the most ultraefficient Preen Machine may be hard put to create even echos from some of the eerie voices that dare cry in the wilderness.

So Many Voters He Didn't Know What To Do

In its origin, there was a method to the identification madness. (Now there seems to be more madness in the method.) In the beginning, even until early man, recognition was for one purpose: to establish order, peace, and progress. It worked. Telling friend from foe, leader from follower, was evolution's insurance for keeping political chaos and larceny to a minimum and cannibalism and mayhem to a bare necessity. It was important to your future whether the animal or man approaching would kiss or kill you. In a buffalo herd or an aborigine tribe, *getting to know you* by the primitive means of sight and smell was the way it was done. Familiarity bred content.

The trick was simply to keep the flocks, packs, and tribes to a size where everyone knew everyone else. A baboon chief knows fact and foible about each and every one of his troop (up to about fifty), and they in turn know his; both understand each other's weaknesses and strengths. There are no strangers, therefore no secrets, and few fears. But when the troop grew over its optimum fifty, there was too much for even the facile-brained baboon to remember. Strangers (not just lovers) appeared in their midst, and who knows about strangers? The troop never got to a hundred because the good common sense of survival came to the rescue. As the excess saw the problems they caused, they simply got themselves a new leader, broke off, and struck out on their own—both groups living happily ever after.

But today everywhere is so full that if an excess wanted to break off, there would be no place to go. If a hundred thousand citizens left Chicago, they would only go to Los Angeles or New York and would still be strangers.

Today's human politician can't recognize many more of his fellows than the baboon can of his. If he'd have been smart, he'd have taken a page from that simian's book and kept things small and manageable. But how could the lowly baboon left in the dust millions of years ago possibly advise that big man with the big brain? And how could a nice little homonid politician from a primitive savannah campsite (brain and all) dream that someday he would have so many constituents he wouldn't know what to do? Could even Nostradamus have predicted that the busy, extroverted politician would become anonymous because there were more voters than could crowd into that cave or campsite?

The Political Frankenstein

Knowing the importance of being important to the politician, even Dante's Seventh Circle of the Inferno, where politicians (all sodomites, no less) serve their penance by running naked through a desert of sand with a rain of fire falling about them, would be heaven compared to their real hell on earth—anonymity. On the other hand, that new solution for anonymity, the shiny new Preen Machine, may yet dig the lone politician into a hotter circle with an even more unendurable punishment, wishing he were back in the relative cool of the Seventh.

How could early political man, without the benefit of staff, demographers, and sociologists, know that bigger, better, and more was worse? How could he have foreseen the need for a machine to broadcast his virtues farther than the powers of his larynx could ever reach? Could it have been foretold that his energy, talent, and intuition, which once spelled his fame and fortune, would someday be only the raw (frequently red-raw) material and that he would have to be refined, remolded, and recast into a sign of our times? So, as in pollution or traffic, politics improvised with each emergency (as it still does), and as the "selling of the candidate" became necessary, so did the Preen Machine.

But the politician's problems don't start way down in Dante's Hell, they start right here on the uppercrust. He'll just have to deal with the hereafter when he gets there as any other political exigency. Here and now, even the poorest politician can't do without his Preen Machine. Exorbitant as an SST and as difficult to service as a Rolls-Royce, it runs only on that superoctane unfossilized energizer, *money.* This good ferry must be kept up to the minute with every new gadget to help carry it across messy political quagmires, with enough power to float it out if it gets stuck. Every conceivable design and model is now on the market, from Humphrey's Edsel to Nixon's Missile Master.

Was It Rube or Arthur's?

Even Larry O'Brien, one of the inventors of this Frankenstein, is wary of its moods. It is temperamental and erratic and can rise to destroy its own master. In the gubernatorial race in New York State in 1970, Nelson Rockefeller should have at least made some of the monthly payments on Arthur Goldberg's machine—it did so well for Rocky. It would appear that it was built by Arthur's cousin Rube, for every time he opened his mouth or appeared on TV, boxing gloves (a) hit him in both eyes; when he shook a hand it was manacled by handcuffs (b); and when he got up to speak, the trap door (c) was sprung and he disappeared. (The last should have happened early in the campaign.) It was either the machine or the candidate—in any event, it was a disaster.

Some Classical Models

Any politician still unconvinced of the necessity for these miracle machines need only recall the JFK experience. Long before this personable (but mediocre) U.S. senator was an out-and-out presidential candidate, he had a sixteen-cylinder juggernaut getting more headlines, pictures, documentaries, and talk shows than the then-president, Eisenhower. Kennedy's vehicle could upstage Ike at a VFW convention. (It's known now that the Salinger/O'Donnell/O'Brien "cream" machine was tuned better for public relations than for political performance.) Even LBJ, the old "do it yourself" backyard mechanic, had a pretty good homemade model going for him, but he insisted on changing carburetors (Moyers, Reedy, Christian, Valenti) every time the engine missed.

Richard Nixon took the machine from the Model T prototype into the electronic and Wankel age. He souped up a new rotary engine (with a minimum of movable parts) and made it totally controllable—even to a gyrating plastic radiator cap in the form of Ron Ziegler, wired for sound and manipulated to action by pushbutton remote control. *In toto,* it was first assembled and (before Watergate) greased and gassed daily by J. Walter Thompson Associates and their supermechanic Haldeman or Ehrlichman the moonlighting plumber. It was a spanking new efficiency job, no demonstrator (Nixon didn't trust demonstrators). It had only a few overt bugs. It heated up too easily with friction. It consumed too much (nonfossil) fuel. It always veered to the right, tended to be a bit balky going up the Hill, and was difficult to polish (even by the press). But so far, it has gotten them where they want to go. The real test will be the Watergate 500 finale. There are omens that this particular Preen Machine may ultimately break down in one big heap like the One-Horse Shay.

Replaceable Parts

Some of the newer models have hidden parts (always replaceable) which may help rev up the political RPM. For instance, there are the superchargers like Nixon aide Charles Colson whose special functions ranged from dirty tricks to the alleged super-spy Hunt's burglary of the Ellsberg files. As Colson declared so vividly neither sleet nor rain nor running over his poor old grandmother could deter him from his (disappointing) rounds.

Then there are the fuel-injector "pens for hire" like the gummy Clark Mollenhoff, the malleable and friction-softened Richard Goodwin, and William Safire, a whimsical part that chokes without lots of "fuel." For a fee, these parts will put into political prose or poetry anything from an inaugural address to a one-liner for almost any customer.

Another easily replaceable part is the special nonself-effacing academic plugs that seem to work without *points.* Prima donna parts like the J. K. Galbraiths and A. Schlesinger, Jr., consider their parts greater than the whole. They haven't as yet heard that they are obsolete and inefficient in the new rotary model (with only one function to a part) even with their efficiency credentials, if not ratings. They are generally ineffectual in influencing their intellectual colleagues, much less Middle America. With more wit than wisdom on practically any subject, their pontification produces nauseous polluting exhausts that are easily detectable, and at times noxious to the candidate's political health. Entranced with their own image, they are typical of their forbears—the din-making, howling monkeys who scream more to announce their own presence than that of their leaders.

Would You Buy A Used . . .

The designer of most of the high-styled, custom-made models is also the general jack-of-all-trades, the Image Maker. He is not only a supersalesman, but also an all-purpose mechanic, troubleshooter, and test driver. (In reality, he is no more than a mechanically inclined Amos and Andy soap salesman who uses social science and machinery to bring it all together.) Like any good service manager, he strikes fear into the hearts of the slack-jawed candidate with tongue-twisting psychosocial terminology, drawing ghastly pictures of the fatal accidents that will surely occur without his ultrasafe, steel-belted, road-gripping speeches for slippery political slopes, or his think-battery that will start in the dead of a campaign winter. These hypersalesmen (of the used-car variety) work on the correct assumption that politicians are afraid *not* to have a modern-styled this-year's model when they have so far to go so soon.

The Image Maker knows his customer will pay to have his supergenes displayed most effectively (and holds the keys till he does). The more paid, of course, the better portrayed.

The new political gurus like miracle worker Joe Napolitan, Garth, or Ailes are in the business of projecting the "little man who wasn't there"—from mayor to presidents, often pride themselves on creating a winning statesman from an ego junkyard. So far, their track record is spotty. Napolitan made his (now shaky) reputation on taking a wizened little Philadelphia electronics salesman, Milton Shapp, and by reprinting a million dollars of his circuits made him governor of Pennsylvania (on the second time around). But the circuits were almost shot before they were used, and from the looks of it, he is destined to return to the one-term junk heap, circuits and all. (In any event he has about as much know how in running Harrisburg as a ditch-digger has for brain surgery.) Two tough mayoral foxes, Frank Rizzo, the cop who flunked his lie detector test, and Pete Flaherty, the independent maverick in Pittsburgh, among other Quaker State pros look at Shapp and lick their grinning chops with only one problem among them—who'll get the drumstick and who'll get the neck.

It's dubious how much these supercircuit-makers can, by their new techniques, promote good political genes, or how far they can boost poor ones. It's strange that the not immodest Napolitan has been unusually silent on the results of his latest media campaigns or his Preen advice to his own silent partner Larry O'Brien during the postconvention maelstrom when Larry lost both his job and his pride. Nor does Robert Squier (now the new image man for Robert Strauss and the Democratic National Committee) regale his colleagues and the press with tales of his successes with Senator Ed Muskie on the back of a platform truck in snowy New Hampshire.

Eye-Ball Genetics and Digit Delphics

Among themselves, when these purveyors of campaign schlock let down their hair, they admit that they can only gild the lily, not doctor the gene (at least not as yet). Their principal technique is eyeball genetics. They size up the stuff as it is, polish what they can, and cover what they must. Sometimes they have to hold some heads underwater or keep them caged to make them *household words*. Others may have to be purged and bled, and occasionally surgery must be undergone to fuse a sagging spine (frequently, though, only a brain transplant would help). Even a titanium-tooled Preen Machine can't create political life. At best, it can only bring the basic political gene up to its potential (or down to its true incompetence). As Ailes, the Nixon packager, let slip in a weaker moment: "One does the best he can with what he has to work with" (he must have had the vision of Bernadette to have performed that once in a lifetime Lourdes-like miracle with RMN).

Besides their mumbo jumbo and plastic surgery, these political impressarios also use various and sundry technicians like Gallup, Harris, and Scammon—the old Delphic Oracles revisited. Going under the guise of social or political analysts, they've created a new numbers racket—"adjusting" the respected digit to the business at hand. Legitimized Jeane Dixons of the political world, they use their modern polling techniques in feats of mathematical legerdemain that would awe Pythagoras, Whitehead, or Houdini.

By the appropriate (or improper) questionnaires, a bit of computer programming, some calculating calculus, and a murky crystal ball, they can come up with whatever the political doctor orders—not only predicting trends, but making them. They have the capacity to change questionnaires or leak results, inject hope or manufacture despair, make or break candidates. Not that they would, especially when the issue is of a nonelective nature. With such issues as how people feel about NATO, female rights, or *The Last Tango in Paris*, they are 99 percent accurate. When it's politics, that's another story; they may fall closer to McGovern's 1,000 percent. True to the nature of their talent, like the carnival barker or a shifty street vendor, by the time the trick is sold, they, their mathematical election trivia, and their fold-up stands are around the corner and far away—forgotten until next time.

It's said that pollsters are only human, and though figures may not be biased, the biased may figure. Ideologic leanings or interesting incentives take their objectivity toll even among the true-blue pollsters. Though they deal only with the immutable digit, it's hardly *à la Descartes*, and the digit is not left unscathed. Adding machines, computers, and comptometers are fine, but greater love hath no man for the old-fashioned cash register than these galluping seers.

Nevertheless, the pollsters aren't all political and they can be objective (even accurate), especially in their final-minute predictions, which are too late to help or hurt, but by which they are judged. Six days before the California primary of 1972, it was leaked (with, of course, no intention to influence) that HHH was an impossible twenty points behind McGovern. Not one reporter believed it but all printed it in inch-high headlines.

Support, contributions, and morale began to fade like friends from an indicted vice president. Even so, in the final vote, HHH was beaten by less than 5 percent.

The Siamese Candidate

The Preen Machine's effectiveness is partly due to its versatility. It has four gears forward, two in reverse, and on occasion it tunnels its way underground—passenger and all. Every eventuality is anticipated. Were the candidate in the nature of a Siamese twin or a Cyclops, the machine could rise to the occasion, repackaging, merchandising, carrying him (or it) to a back-to-back victory with one-eyed jacks. Frequently, a candidate is better heard than seen; all the blue shirts, capped-tooth smiles, and teleprompters in the world can't put some of those Humpty Dumptys together for the TV tube. For them, TV is more giant-killer than king-maker.

In Richard Nixon's case, where there was more to be hidden, the Preen Machine hid it. With all of the soft touches the Democrats served up to him in 1968 (Chicago, Gene McCarthy, academic riots, principled liberals, and antiwar fat cats), he still almost blew it by his few inimitable TV appearances. As probably the most unloved presidential candidate since U. S. Grant or Calvin Coolidge, every thirty-second spot was guaranteed to lose a dozen precincts, even in his beloved Orange County, California. Taking no chances in 1972, he might as well have been a five-o'clock-shadowed troglodyte, allowed only to roam subterranean passages, safe from the probing electronic eye. His métier was the faceless radio, where he was heard, but not seen.

To See Himself As Mother Sees Him

To expose or not to expose, that is the question. If, as the saying goes, TV reveals political character, there may not be enough of it around to squander all that money on. Recognition has two charges, positive and negative, attraction and repulsion, and it can go either way. In other words, if TV doesn't lie, it can only hurt, so why bother? Bother? It's no bother, not to the preeners anyway, not when buying time alone coins a cool 15 percent (not including expenses and production costs). Even if TV exposure might be hazardous to a candidate's health (and not by its radiation), if the preeners want to continue to wade in the drippings, they have to bring home a candidate's political bacon first.

The smart media finaglers' motto is: "Identification without revelation." But that's a hard idea to sell to a candidate who loves to see himself as Mother sees him. Using only his name and face blinked on and off a thousand times an hour like a neon sign a hundred times is better and cheaper than the deadly ego trip biographies. It would give recognition without insight, possibly create a winner, and in the bargain, not lower the venal vendor's comfortable living standard too much.

But with the candidate's ego, plus the king-maker's faith in his own infallibility, the best-laid plans of mice and hucksters go awry. What little is naturally going for a candidate can frequently be ruined. Exposure has often led to political asthma, which is frequently fatal. The most recent tubal casualties were Muskie and McGovern, two overexposed *negatives* with no proofs positive.

Whistler's Mother, Cornball Klunkers, and Such

Ed Muskie's bid for the big one was concocted from one folksy Lincolnesque telecast in 1970. Taking this lone success as the trademark for the campaign, that same style was repeated nationwide in his announcement to run. It was all over before it started. Creative image-maker Bob Squier Lincolnesqued Muskie right back to the Senate. Staged in a homey Kennebunkport, Maine, cabin, rocking away by a cheery fireplace, Muskie needed only a shawl to be Whistler's mother in drag. It turned off every voter under the grandmotherly age and there weren't enough left over to win a New Hampshire primary.

Tireless, McGovern was; tubeless, he should have been. In him, the recyclers had a TV challenge that defied plastic surgery or technology. It is difficult in any national election to lose forty-nine states, but he did it despite the film genius of Charles Guggenheim. If he had had no TV exposure at all, he could have lost only one more. Trying to "Madison Avenue" up one of the sweetest cornball klunkers ever to hold national office was an Augean stable Hercules would have sent to the cleaners. Attempting to convert McGovern's cadaverous style, back-country nasal delivery, and Mortimer Snerd facial characteristics into a tough dynamic leader-image was flouting nature itself.

In 1970 and again in 1972, recyclers had just as impossible a job distilling the nitric acid ruthlessness of that great California legislator, Jesse Unruh, into a sweet California Manischewitz Concord.

Even the Preen Machine, in its present state of technical proficiency, can't make feet of clay walk on water.

Raterdamerung

So the fruits of billions of years of evolution, which worked out a perfectly good system of using identification as a means toward life, liberty, and the pursuit of property, had to be "modernized." There is no doubt modernization has done wonders in projecting the candidate. But what about the system? Is the voter now alienated because of it, and can there be "no representation without alienation"? Can the Preen Machine sell, brainwash, project, convince, and inspire well enough not only to elect a candidate, but also to keep the natives from getting restless?

If the experiments at the National Institute of Mental Health (in the Laboratory of Brain Evolution and Behavior, under Dr. John B. Calhoun) are any criteria, our angels had better look homeward. The Preen Machine may presage a twilight of the mods.

Dr. Calhoun proved that a mouse society gradually dies when it grows so large that there is no longer mutual recognition—mouse to leader, leader to mouse. He started one colony with just four males and four females under ideal Miami Beach-like conditions—rich, well-fed, and content. Each mouse had his own kith, kin, and role within the cage community, at least for awhile. But those little communicating cage villages grew naturally into massive mice megalopoli. Then the trouble began. When the colony reached four to six hundred, the mice leaders couldn't begin to know all of their followers and the followers couldn't tell a leader without a score card. At about population twelve to fifteen hundred, there was no identity at all, follower to leader or friend to enemy, and confrontations and riots were reminiscent of the Berkeley campus. The mice began attacking each other because it was the surest way of not being killed. In this mouse bedlam, the young became inert and autistic; soon they could neither defend themselves nor even mate. In just four years, all twenty-two hundred of the colony were dead. Because of the loss of the (identification) nail, a rat society was lost.

It Can't Happen Here

If rodent psychology can be extrapolated to voters and politicians (and why not?—we use rats to help solve many other human ills), we'd better think hard on how to stuff three billion of us back into manageable tribes and caves. If the rats aren't warning enough, maybe Watergate is, for if ever a Preen Machine did its duty, it was in 1968 and 1972.

But this can't happen here. We have a Constitution, a Congress, and a Supreme Court; an Environmental Protection Agency, a Small Business Administration, the CIA, and others to see that it won't. We must have faith, faith in those same wonderful leaders who in the past have given us smog, inflation, the assembly lines, food additives, and the New Politics. And we must have trust in that same human electorate that gave us leaders like Harding, Coolidge, and Agnew. And last but not least, we must believe in the Preen Machine as we believe in its first cousin that sells us stuff that keeps us regular, clears our sinuses, and reassures us that Preparation H will do the job. Though the problems may seem insurmountable, the Preen Machine is yet in its infancy. Who knows, if it doesn't break down (and why should it, its cousin is still healthy after a hundred years), it may go on to bigger and better things and do away with the candidate altogether.

X

The Paper Tigers

(*The Wayward Mutant*)

> The average newspaperman, especially of the better sort, has the intellect of a hillbilly evangelist, the courage of a rat, the fairness of a prohibitionist boob, the information of a high school janitor, the taste of a designer of celluloid Valentines and the honor of a police station lawyer.
>
> —H. L. MENCKEN

The strangest and most aggravating phenomenon plaguing the already overplagued politician is the omnipresent, if not omniscient, Fourth Estate. A politician's dream world is incomplete without a press conference *sans* reporters; just a lovely one-way conference with cameras and microphones, but no press. For if there was ever a double, reciprocal genetic xenophobia, it's between the politician and the press. As Dr. Hunter S. Thompson, that master of freaked-out four-letter-word journalism so aptly cadged and warmed over from journalists like Mencken and Shaw, "One of the main marks of success in a career politician is a sooty distrust of the press," a feeling reciprocated in spades by every right-thinking reporter. But where a politician or reporter stands usually depends on where he sits. During his presidency, Thomas Jefferson said, "Nothing can be believed which is in a newspaper." In retirement, when the heat was off, he mellowly stated, "The press is the best instrument for enlightening the mind of man."

John P. Gadfly

This genial relationship dates back to the first journalist and seems to have been carefully cultivated on both sides ever since.

Right off the bat some ten thousand years ago, when this mutant breed suddenly appeared on the phylogenetic scale (as if by spontaneous generation), embarrassing the politicians has been its stock in trade. Beginning in the Lascaux Caves, the reporter started by painting nasty pictures on the walls showing the early leader as a bumbler. Later, the Hieroglyphic Courier-Journal depicted Cleopatra's pompous and greedy political henchmen no differently than the modern poison pen portrays them. The politician has never taken this lying down, but for all the good it's done him, he might as well have.

Like any other group (dogs, cats, ITT executives, or Republicans), members of this subspecies, the press, are drawn together by the similarity of their genes, which in itself is remarkable, considering their less than lovable professional character and equally questionable personal habits which should even repel each other. But as such, they are a part of the political evolutionary process. Though their function seems rather obscure to the naked eye, it appears that their *raison d'être* is to interpret the leader to the follower—though not always precisely the way the leader sees it.

There must have been some special problems between politician and follower around 8000 B.C., the particular time in biologic history that the press first emerged. For before that, the leaders and followers had been suffering each other tolerably well for some billions of years without the benefit of reporters. From the evidence so far, this disjointed venture has had its ups and downs, and from the looks of it, either the politician or the reporter must go. The odds are six, two, and even it won't be the politician.

No Origin of this Species

Thus, hanging in Limbo as a go-between for constituent and politician, and being so young (10,000 or so years), this new breed has been difficult to figure out. They may not last long enough to make the effort worthwhile, for they are highly specialized and we know that specialized species like the whooping crane and the albino pygmy are threatened by the slightest environmental change. Their demise may be no great loss to society (according to some of our best politicians), but while they're still with us they are of scientific interest. They seem to have arisen from nowhere, they have no visible origin, no umbilicus to speak of.

Ordinarily, a species or subspecies can readily be traced back to its beginning: such as the human to the little tree shrew; and the politician to any one of the many reptilian orders. Discounting the Renaissance theory of spontaneous generation or the biblical one of Adam's rib, even Theodosius Dobzhansky, the outstanding genetic sleuth and philosopher, would be hard put to trace the political press back to its animal origin. The behavioral patterns and idiosyncrasies (its lust for power and especially its voyeuristic compulsion) leave no alternative but to conclude that this excrescence on the body politic has no known derivation as even the sea slug has. The amphibious crocodile could have been predicted from the aquatic shark, and the free-swinging politician from the tree-swinging baboon. But reporters seem to bear no relationship to any known primordial creature flying, crawling, or amphibious.

Though one is a firm believer in Darwin's theories, the mystery of the journalist's genealogy brings mythical creatures to mind. When one thinks of publishers, the metaphoric facsimile of the lugubrious dragon, its thick, scaley skin (impervious to the spear of any political St. George), its soft white belly (mopping up the dirt), its nostrils belching more smoke than fire, seems related. The well-tailored hard-driving editors remind one of the graceful unicorn, its shapely equine head extruding a tough spiral horn from a superthick cranium that could gut a rhinoceros. Even more appropriately the happy-go-lucky roving political reporters (or especially photographers) could most easily be throwbacks to the devilish satyr; bacchanalian in spirit, full of the sauce of the grape, piping his haunting melodies as he chases the female with fun and fervor (especially on a foreign assignment), yet with cloven hoofs as facile as kicking a quarry senseless as dancing the night away.

Nevertheless, as a group (especially reporters), hints of a higher primate may show through, as in a troop of bright-eyed, young macaque monkeys lined up on a limb, transfixed by the adult world beneath them. With furrowed brows, they worriedly peer at the drama below; with quick inquisitive glances at each other, they are ready to stay or switch, whichever the group decides. When they have seen enough or their limited attention span wanes, they set up a din of chatter as if broadcasting the results, then go into euphoric motion, clasping each other and swinging wildly through the trees.

These simian antics are almost duplicated by the brotherhood of political voyeurs. One can see them in Joe Kraft, Tom Wicker, and Dan Rather as they silently watch, listen, and scribble away on the periphery of a press conference, then, with the "Thank you, Mr. Senator, Congressman, etc," explosively dash to the phones and typewriters to chatter away to the waiting world. Finally, arms around each other's shoulders, they head for their boozy breather at a nearby watering hole.

Peeping Tomism

Voyeurism, the most common trait of the profession, is uncommon in animals. The owl, the panther, and the chimpanzee may like nothing better than to sit unseen, either quizzically or gleefully watching how the other half disport themselves, but the more prideful animals are above this sort of nosey pastime. However, the political reporter has somehow elevated this spectator sport to that of professional peeping tomism, making a passable living at it to boot. Spying on the antics of another subspecies may be carrying a minor genetic trait a little too far, but one can't say they haven't made the most of it. Where on the phylogenetic scale does one find another species, living or dead, that can survive on such a thin pretext?

In their role between politician and follower, they have developed a keen and perceptive sense of the trivial, the prurient, and the macabre—which, as they say, "sells newspapers," or network commercials. They have managed to keep their principal patron, the follower, amused if not educated, for they've found that their gentle reader is interested in what brand of ketchup President Nixon uses on his cottage cheese or whether John Kennedy really slept without pajama bottoms and is Senator Claiborne Pell from Rhode Island still tied to his mother's apron strings. Of course, no newspaper pro gives in completely to this type of investigative reporting and here and there intersperses filler of a more substantive political nature to round out a story. On occasion (a two in seventeen hundred shot), a Woodward and Bernstein may break with tradition and show something beyond the usual political gossip and rumor.

The Eyes of the Beholder

Because there are few geneologic clues along the evolutionary trail, the reporter is even a bit confused about himself, and he should be, hanging suspended like a misbegotten child with no known past and a shaky future. Psychologically he overcompensates for his lack of a navel engagement by fobbing himself off as an urbane man of letters in the public service, a recorder of history, witty, objective, an individualist to his eyeteeth. The politician views him in a somewhat less civilized light, more like a prying little man from Mars with a small pointy head sprouting a revolving radar screen; protruding, searching eyes on flexible stems and the index finger of the right hand a dripping source of ink. The truth may be somewhere in between these specious speculations by the involved parties. It may be more fruitful and altogether less tiring to identify some of the better known journalistic specimens and the species they most closely resemble in order to give a hint of the basic characteristics (if any) of the journalist.

For instance, the saturnine, lazy-lipped David Brinkley must have sprung whole from the duck-billed platypus family. And the smirking Bill Buckley could not but be related to the ferretlike mongoose, toying with his natural enemy, the liberal cobra. "Scotty" Reston, a pipe-smoking, wise (or otherwise) old owl looks with superior disdain from his olympian "tree tops" at the likes of Evans and Novak, a breed of Wasp-and-Polish hyena snuffling below in the deserted campsite garbage. One can see Joseph Alsop's resemblance to the mantis family, in his foppish pale-green elegance, out on a limb, praying in posture, but preying in nature with the civilized demeanor of a lady bug but the crushing mandibles of a carnivor.

Katharine Graham and Dorothy Schiff—queens of the phalaropes—have the identical dominant characteristics of their

South African feathered friend, one of the few of their sex calling the tune as they peddle the word.

Tom Wicker, a chipmunk with cheeks puffed full of juicy political nuts, yet still nibbling away at his own hangup. Art Buchwald's ancestors could have been descended from none other than the jovial fin-clapping walrus, crushing political ego by his sheer fun-loving weight.

The Flabby Tabby

It is said that the press personality gravitates to politics mainly by default. (It couldn't be money.) What other congeries of living conflicts like reporters would aspire to make a living off the self-aggrandizing, self-expiating, egomanical politicians, whose principal aim is to cover-up, fuzz, and obfuscate in speciously worded Xeroxed releases at pettifogging press conferences?

On the other hand, what kind of quirky mind then enjoys peeling off, adding to, mixing fact and fancy, guessing, conjecturing, coloring, or discounting those releases for the sole purposes of explaining to a mass of lexophobics limited to headlines, pictures, and cartoons.

It's something more than a last resort. Reporters can't be accused of just filling a vacuum everyone else abhors any more than the politicians they dog. They're both attracted by the same lure—power.

It Takes One to Know One

Though they appear a happy-go-lucky, free-wheeling lot, constantly deploring power and politics, political reporters are power-ridden only a little less than their political meal ticket. (As it's said, it takes one to know one.) If they weren't they would be writing gossip, science, or even sports, all of which are easier, less hectic, and better-paid subjects than politics.

Actually, they are frustrated politicians. Frustrated not that they love power less, but they love security more and can't have both. That's why they're in the name not the game.

Actors, lawyers, and candlestick-makers may take the political plunge, and even make it. But though newsmen like Novak, Douglas Kiker, or Dan Rather appear to have all the natural overbearance, arrogance, and insensitivity it takes to be an elected official, they never chance it. It takes a spine stiffer than soggy newsprint and a heart stouter than a paper-pulp pump to play double or nothing. Roaring, stalking, and clawing at the quaking quarry they'd love to be, the paper tiger sheaths his fangs if the comfort of that steady paycheck or that pension at the end of the long, long tunnel, is endangered.

They love to watch and eloquently rapture over the warm glow of the hearth at a distance, but like other beasts, they are deadly afraid of the *heat of the kitchen*. When all ovens were fired up in the old Nixon-Agnew cookout of the *effete, snobbish, Eastern liberal press*, the networks (even the public broadcasters) had to be led out of the red-hot kitchen blindfolded. All of those honorable men, CBS's Stanton, NBC's Goodman, and ABC's Goldenson, cozied up to the White House as publishers from Knight in Miami to Chandler in Los Angeles began handling Nixon as if he were a Wedgwood heirloom. Also, not to be half-safe, the tired blood of the Sulzberger *Times* went so far as to hire an in-house writer, William Safire, from 1600 Pennsylvania Avenue. But Watergate set them free unsheathing the claws again.

Actually, the hearts of these paper tigers could have been heartier and their spines firmer, for they were as safe as if they were in the Bronx Zoo (or better, a protected source). When the chips are down, whether it's the Pentagon Papers, Jack Anderson's grand jury sources, payola, or Evans and Novak as Ron Ziegler's *out-house* leaks, they *plead the First* no differently than the Mafia pleads the Fifth. A. J. Liebling, one of their own, stuck it to them—"freedom of the press belongs to those who own one." And yea, though they walk (or run amok) through the valley of the shadows of political power, they shall fear no evil for their First Amendment rods and their libel law staffs comfort them all the days of their lives.

Old tabby has more built-in protection than the Houston back-up. For she can lob her inkpots over the walls of Fortress Newsprint at the unprotected politician and the only comeback is a letter to the editor defused in fine print. What explanation, denial, or rebuttal could neutralize the inch-high "Muskie Weeps in New Hampshire!" or explain a beautifully arranged front-page picture of Senator "Scoop" Jackson campaigning to two people in a park in the 1972 Florida primary?

Jack Anderson's rare apology (for those nonexistent Eagleton alcoholic binges that blared from page one) had an indecent burial between the obituaries and the church notices. It did as much for the vice presidential nominee as George McGovern's 1,000 percent support.

Unoriginal Sin in the Youngest Profession

As safe and secure as they are, the bedeviled, peripatetic, un-regulated life they lead has some side effects and does take its toll. Just dealing with the machinations of the political brain drives them to drink, sex, and other similar diversions that might mitigate their agony. But though this conditioning contributes to their personal delinquency, case histories show unequivocally that their patterns and habits were not only prevalent before they were vocationally trapped, but way before puberty. There is definitely a congenital bent, and their composite history, reeking of precocious libidious and bibulous habits carried over into adulthood, more or less proves it.

This is not to say this breed doesn't have special talents; unfortunately, they may not be in the field of writing. Even so, there has stumbled into their midst in the past half-century a literary taint in the originality and style of H. L. Mencken, A. J. Liebling, and Walter Lippmann. But even these mutant-mutants who may have added lustre to the profession were back-bitten and undermined by their overinflated, underachieving colleagues—another example of one of their many unoriginal sins.

Which is not to say reporters are characterless. The exceptional traits of the press may not be legion, and the parrotlike knack to copy down and recite back may be no mean feat (especially if there is an adequate rewrite man chained to the desk), but they are unequivocally goal oriented. If they can keep from making the big mistake of trying to put something of themselves into their work, it is a steady, if subsistance, employment—a goal no one can demean.

The politician should expect little more from the press than what he gets, for the intellectual and moral prerequisites for a reporter are about the same as those for the oldest profession— a natural tendency and an eye to survival. They even drift into the game in a similar fashion; usually as dropouts from some other reliable enterprise or profession, or backwater college literati who couldn't hack it in more respectable intellectual pursuits.

Though politicians, too, are usually self-anointed with no special skills, they have the good sense to rarely claim intellectual superiority, clairvoyance, or pure objectivity. Knowing themselves as they do, they cock a wary eye at those denizens of an institution that protests too much. They should expect no more objectivity than from Portnoy's mother nor a fairer shake than from Nathan Detroit's floating crap game—and they get it.

The quality of dogged persistence in seeking the truth has always been a watermark characteristic of the profession. They hang onto an issue or a lead like the Mounties, until they get their man. Watergate was a marvelous journalistic feat, and can't be faulted just because it was little and late. Though only two reporters on one newspaper from among those couple of thousand dailies with their tens of thousands of reporters were convinced it wasn't just a Ziegler-like playful political prank or two-bit burglary; there have been even worse unheeded cries in the wilderness. But they'll not be caught next time around. Even a Teapot Dome or Watergate scandal have their fifty-year cycles.

Then there is pride—pride of individuality for instance. If it shows up nowhere else in his professional life, it does in his haberdashery. The flashy cut and color of his raiment would be the envy of even the flamboyant horn-billed cockatoo.

Even in his work the reporter tries hard to be himself. It's just difficult with what little the close-to-the-vest politician gives him to work with. Yet the reporter's workaday world demands copy and one can understand the sin of journalistic incest worthy of Faulkner's hillbilly Snopese, when an editor's wrath is the alternative. A rumor dropped at the Carousel Bar in Saigon will reach the Crillion in Paris faster than the speed of sound and will be in most morning editions, embellished, analyzed, and finalized in admirable consistency as if written by one hand.

The Care and Feeding of Strange Bedfellows

Though the prevailing opinion in the press is that all politicians are thieves and liars, and the consensus among politicians is that the press is a *gang* of SWINE, these two strange bedfellows comfortably curl around each other like bear cubs in a den. Even that journalistic maverick I. F. (Izzy) Stone, who when once asked about his isolation from smart journalistic circles around powerful men in public life replied, "I've just been isolated from bores and jerks," has himself been known to turn up at cocktail parties and freebies of that sort. It's a natural symbiosis, like the tiny birds who sit safely on the rhino's ear digging out the succulent, nutritious, newsy ticks as the pachyderm sighs with the temporary public relief he gets. No one denies that on a downbeat day the bird may peck a little less kindly and may even draw blood, or the disconcerted political pachyderm may give a nasty twitch of the ear, flinging the journalistic bird into the bush. But, on the whole, they are worse off without each other.

In this mutual desperation society where each tolerates the other, the reciprocal care and feeding strikes a delicate balance. The politician needs his ego pablum sugared and the reporter his exclusives or leaks fermented to his particular savor. In the process, they both bravely bear each other's little eccentricities for the common good.

At the publisher-editor level, it's the social art, not the dietetics of mutual nourishment. During Camelot, Ben Bradlee, editor of the *Post*, Reston of the *Times*, and Huntley of NBC were at the Middleburg bed, board, and booze of JFK more often than they were at the Press Club bar. It was *in*, prestigious, and they enjoyed it, and knowingly or unknowingly paid for it in good press at Waldorf rates. But both parasite and host were satisfied.

On the other hand when the great lords of the press have their feathers ruffled or their egos pricked, they'll strike to ruin.

William Loeb of the *Manchester-Union Leader* knocked Ed Muskie right out of the primary box in 1972 and P. Block the little Napoleon of the Toledo *Blade,* said he wouldn't support HHH in 1968 because Hubert was ten minutes late for breakfast—and he didn't.

For the stiffs of the working press, the Irish Mafia were like the flying Wallendas, keeping sixteen reporters, columnists, and photographers in the air at all times (without a net). Salinger, O'Brien, O'Donnell, and Donahue juggled the timing of issues, leaks, specials, created exclusives, and wined and dined the influential ones, without the benefit of enemy lists, plumbers, the FBI, or Internal Revenue. They did it so well that every Mother's Son of the Lord Goddess Newsprint felt like a yellow cur if he didn't say it just as it was composed for him. To this day, fewer than half of them know they were had—delightfully so, but had.

On the other hand, the Katzenjammer Kids of the Nixon administration had about as much finesse in spoon-feeding as a zookeeper stuffing a python. Having a bourbon and branch with a tight-sphinctered Ziegler was as relaxing as spending the pre-resignation weekend with Spiro Agnew. And the charm of a gourmet lunch of cottage cheese and ketchup just wasn't all that appealing to the expense-account–prone free-loading palates of the Fourth Estate.

Tsetse Fly Romance

Though every reporter likes to feel that there are some friendly natives in the political jungle and every politician likes an inky (if kinky) friend—but even between the best of political friends, the story's the thing. If an editor smells reporter-politician détente, he demands his pound of rancor. In 1967, when confrontation dogged HHH in his vice presidential travels abroad, a telegram came from a wire service to the covering reporter in London to the effect "What's wrong—no riots—confrontation copy needed—next." The reporter may just have had enough of riots, or found them boring, or maybe an ounce of compassion had crept in. But the next story was a beaut—the editor prevailed.

Come what may, working press–politician relations are about as permanent as the short-lived romances of the tsetse fly. The

New Deal, the Fair Deal, Camelot, and the Great Society had honeymoons with their press lovers only so long as the curlers weren't seen at breakfast. The grounds for divorce were more style than substance. Style Camelot had, and she cleverly had breakfast in bed, unseen till high noon; the press knew her only at the ball. On the other hand, the affair with Lyndonlot was short and sweet. The substantive makeup couldn't cover the styleless warts.

There are always open charges by politicians that the press is hostile and press counterclaims that they are only natural adversaries in the public's service. Both are true. But give and take is either better or worse according to who can do what for whom at any particular time. Teddy White has been a particular pet of the Kennedys since the first *Making of the President*, and they have done well by him ever after. (He has now, peculiarly enough, taken a shine to Nixon.) With Joe Alsop, Nixon could do no wrong (until recently) and Alsop in turn got special consideration from him. Marianne Means swooned in print every time Johnson winked at her, and a broad Harvard A crept into Tom Wicker's drawl in 1960. Teddy Kennedy couldn't get to first base with Means; nor LBJ with Wicker.

As in every jungle order there are always some with even less romance than a tsetse fly. These are the few pariahs that even the most animal-loving human couldn't cotton to. They are neither lovable nor loving because they are innately poisonous or repulsive, like a pit adder or a skunk. This type of political reporter or commentator can't help himself for he was born with his venom sack and flatulence organs and gives forth toxins or odors with or without provocation. They know who they are. The most friendly of overtures, or none at all, may be greeted by the most noxious of responses. The politician who clasps one of them to his bosom is like a serpent-handling zealot, neither testing his faith nor his good sense.

The Golden Pollen

The press may not live by bread alone, but their glamor boys have a strong weakness for the doughy long green. They not only need recognition and exposure for their daily bread, but they must also cast it upon the waters and count on its multiplying.

The way to do it is by a sequence of events listed in every "how to succeed" political manual. The more they consort with the politicians, the more they get "in" on the Georgetown dinner circuit and thus have the best sources, with more fresh news, gossip, rumors, breaks, and leads. Then they start appearing on the air (or the front page) more often, thus hiking their income, becoming more familar, and more in demand on the Ladies' Garden Club circuit. That is how they build a constituency and become a force and that's what politicians like to consort with.

These news-gathering butterflies flitting among the political petunias have now become accustomed to stashing away more golden pollen on the way to the dais or the Book-of-the-Month Club than in their daily newsmaking stints.

Racing to Extinction

No doubt the press is a charming anomaly. But as a fresh late-starter with obscure origins, even though it serves a temporary purpose, it's bound to be short-lived in the overall political ecology. For evolution has shown that no highly specialized animal, whether the mammoth or the pterodactyl, survives for long. Journalism may peter out over a long period of time and just become a nuisance, or it may go the whole hog quickly and wind up back in its murky past, never to rise again. The signs are up—"Prepare for Your Maker"—for the paranoid political psyche has had it and the Shield Laws are the openers.

Why should a politician risk his image with a hostile sub-species when by his own brain he can more reliably and consistently create a machine of his own that sees both events and himself exactly as he thinks they should be. It makes things more tidy. *Pravda* and *Tass* were the typesetting on the wall, Latin America followed suit (eighteen out of twenty-one countries have a nicely controlled press), as did Greece, Vietnam, China, and practically all of Africa. And only by the grace of God and the Watergate were Nixon and Agnew temporarily short-circuited in their campaign to even things up. (The solons of the Fourth

Estate should mount plaques in every editorial room in the land to their temporary savior, that Watergate guard.)

All of this may be only a brief respite for what is left of this now endangered subspecies still flourishing only in affluential political climates—like a proud peacock on the manicured lawns of the rich. If it does persist, it will be a feat rivaled by nothing less than the miracle of the three-toed sloth or the wombat. If it doesn't, it will be missed no more than the Anopholes mosquito or the Chigger—at least by that beleaguered soul, the pol.

XI

Playing the System

(*Unchecked and Unbalanced*)

The democratic form of government is the highest form existing and requires the highest type of human nature—which doesn't exist.
—HERBERT SPENCER

The totalitarian form of government requires the lowest form of human nature—which exists in abundance.
—E.F.B.

If pundits from Plato to Cato or Marx to Marcuse had even sniffed the real aroma of power, much less wielded it, or had ever run for anything other than their noonday sherry hours or late-afternoon seminars, we would not now be saddled with their mistaken theories. Had they only observed, they could have learned more about the abnormal psychology of politics from a baboon troop or a precinct captain than from a lifetime within the confines of learned institutions. Marx alone would have had an eye-opener and done a greater service to the Soviets had he spent more time in the English countryside studying a beehive or a herd of Hampshire swine than in the musty British museums learning how the masses were exploited and thinking up ways to get even.

The best those political horticulturists could come up with is a stunted oak with three bare branches: the executive branch, strong but crooked; the legislative, flimsy and quivering; and the judicial limb, frayed and splintered.

This is said in no way to belittle those great political scientists. They were probably well intentioned and had the highest aspirations for a political brain they overestimated and a constituents' brain they didn't estimate at all—not to mention a complete ignorance of the animal origins of their own behavior.

A baboon chief would laugh them out of the ball park if they pulled a fast one like suggesting that the chief's orders be checked by a senate of his own betas or allowing a few of his own political appointees to a court to pass judgment on one of his rulings. But most of all, the baboon would have been shocked that the political scientists would allow the weakest and low-liest omega to have a say (an equal say, mind you) on not only who would lead, but who would make the rules all play by, including the chief.

Round Pegs in Square Systems

If those political specialists who devise systems had had better insight they may have seen the error of their ways early, repented, and left politics to the politicians. But they not only had little knowledge of the animal world, they had only a speaking acquaintance with the real world. Any two-bit ward boss knows that it's tough enough having an Oxford don live up to the UN charter, much less a loinclothed betelnut-chewing tribesman from Swaziland. They may have done better with dolphins.

One of the first laws of political dynamics is that you can't stuff round constituents into square systems. Yet in their brilliance, protected from all reasonable influences, those political philosophers drew up their political blueprints on the assumption that the profile of the common man is a reflection of Leonardo da Vinci rather than austrolopithecus—our first ancestor. They forgot incidentals such as evolution and genetics—as if the average constituent sprang fully formed from a seashell. It's romantic, but romance is about as foreign to politics as a Uzbek peasant is to the court of St. James's. Better they had taken their archetype from the burly, undershirted, dues-paying member-in-good-standing of the Boilermakers' Union, with beer, booze, broads, and baseball on his mind rather than the balance of payments and the First Amendment.

On second thought, maybe those political theorists weren't so well intentioned. No learned cabal, no matter how unani-

mous its political ignorance, could have conjured up, without
malice aforethought, such subtle mischief onto both the politician and the constituent. On the basis of the results alone,
had those learned (if somewhat diabolic) thinkers had a shred
of conscience among them they would have donned their hair-
shirts and gone on hands and knees to Mecca to seek forgiveness
and solace.

Befogged by Revelation—Entranced by Misconception

Disregarding the guilt or innocence of our mentors, we are
stuck with two major systems (at this point in time) under
which we suffer. The one, the conventional democratic myth-
ology, is enraptured by an idealistic fancy for the common man
and the myth of the politician as superman. The other system,
the growing totalitarian gospel, is convinced of the opposite:
that all men (politicians excepted) are little more than mechanisms that can be wound up, given a start, and off they go—
all in step.

In the first instance, the later-day students of society (Jefferson, Adams, et al.), in some sort of epileptic revelation, saw
both voter and leader properly winged and haloed, living by a
divine set of golden rules in Eden. They had obviously not
heard about the incident there with the apple. If they were to
come back to reality, these visionaries with their inch-thick con-
cave lenses ideologically befogged would be shocked to see
voters throwing beer bottles and tomatoes at their leaders, or
even shooting them down. They would be even more dismayed
at the likes of a noble politician like the gentle George Mc-
Govern, as his lofty rhetoric evaporated in frustration, angrily
telling an ordinary run-of-the-mill heckler where he could go
and what he could kiss.

While such high-blown misconceptions of modern democracy
were gradually being perfected, an equal and opposite miscon-
ception was evolving under its very nose. Marx, Engels, and Lenin
thought they were bringing a great boon to mankind with the
system under which the other half now struggles. These earthy
gentlemen not only gave short shrift to the fallacy of the

nobility of the human spirit and the potential of the human brain, but they also convinced a hundred million kulaks and serfs that they are no more than a combination of salts, metals, and other inorganic elements and should whirr and produce like any other turbine or refrigerator.

The efficient apparatchik is naturally in charge and has every right to punish any human frailty that creeps in and cuts down on mechanical efficiency. What right has a generator to a vodka hangover on Monday morning or a toss in the hay during a coffee break on the collective? (Unless, of course, he is a Lenin hero and way over his assigned quota.) And why shouldn't these turbines with uncontrolled animalistic survival instincts who bribe or embezzle (for a possible rainy day) be sent to a Siberian R and R camp? The Soviets claim these well-programmed Eastern turbines are freer, happier, and more productive than those built in the West.

If Marx had been smarter and had gone back to the phylogenetic scale, which man painfully climbed in his evolution, instead of to the old political drawing board, he would have known that even the 100 percent genetically programmed ants he obviously worshipped can occasionally go off on a spree when the system gets on their nerves or stash a grain or two away for a rainy day.

Both the stripped-to-the-middle Middle American of the Silent Majority and the Lenin medal winners for Toilet Bowl Corperatives are very round constituents in the squarest of systems. But each tries to prove that the scheme he labors under is the best when neither is fitted for either.

A System of Wrecks and Parlances

But however misconceived this relationship is between the constituent and the leader, the theoretical relationship among the leaders themselves is even more botched. Not knowing the political gene, our political philosophers didn't understand that all political leadership is divided into two parts totally different from each other. One is the elected official, a photophiliac who loves light, especially the lime kind, and the other is the party politician, who is as photophobic as a ground mole. Every democratic political system must, therefore, have one part out front for show and the working part—the party part—somewhere back in the shadows. (It's said that any machine politician exposed to sunlight and fresh air for over forty-eight hours at a time comes down with a syndrome that renders him a political paraplegic.)

So the systems the political philosophers installed out in the open, though having noble purposes, perfect forms, and being beautiful to behold, could never govern. But leaving nothing to chance, so that governance would never be excellent, they built in a cyclic process that changes leadership so often that the fundamentals of governing can never be learned—assuring chaos.

Whatever his diabolic mood when he conceived the philosophy of a system, the political scientist must have been on a hilarious drunken spree to have foisted on us his method of governance. Imagine the fun he had dreaming up plans in which the politicians not only control themselves, but also each other, and in the process make and execute laws. How could anyone take this with a straight face? Proposing that three coequal branches of government—the executive, legislative, and judicial —work separately but together is like throwing a fresh young gazelle carcass to a coequal group of hungry hyenas, panthers, and tigers. It boded just what we've gotten—lacerated bodies, confused minds, and a kind of government too ludicrous to mention.

Just the idea of checks and balances among politicians must have had them rolling on the floor. Imagine that unholy alliance of executive legislator, and judge checking or balancing anything, much less themselves.

Then take that other prank—the separation of powers. It separates so well that it divides itself and is conquerable from within mainly by number 1—the executive. Its most useful function today seems to be keeping the present executive branch in the driver's seat and it's leader out of jail.

As the father of our country said (but no one would listen), "Government is not reason, is not eloquence—it is force." When it's all boiled down, even with the iron-clad tripartite product of political genius—the careful checks and balances—and the absolute separation of powers guaranteeing a more perfect union, it works no differently than an average baboon troop: by one-man rule. Despite all the effulgent rhetoric as to its perfection, two of the three branches of this government could disappear and not only would never be missed, but would relieve the only one that governs—the executive—from having to carry their load. It's the president (like any baboon leader) who picks his staff, his cabinet, and his agencies, and he doesn't leave anything to the chancy electorate to meddle in nor the nosey Congress to foul up. He knows what he wants done and knows who can do it. He rules like any other jungle monarch and the Congress protestingly knuckles under like any other group of baboon betas.

The Most Equal Executive Branch

If there is any doubt as to who keeps the show on the road and who cracks the whip, simply watch Richard Nixon (with all of his Watergate and vice presidential troubles) putting Congress through flaming hoops by using just a few of the many persuaders in his executive bag of tricks. The veto, the budget, impounding funds, White House invitations, or simply a ride to the home hustings on *Air Force One* are some of the little favors that make a legislator present his hindquarters and bow in deference. It doesn't take much. If worse comes to worst the executive executes. At his lowest ebb, with a Democratic Congress and his popularity down near that of the Manson family, RMN has so far been sustained seven times on vetoes by that independent, individualistic body of lawmakers.

Psychologically, the democratic system is like putting three prima donnas in one trio, and expecting to hear a virtuoso performance. Since when would Beverly Sills *sotto voce* for Maria Callas? And since when would a majority leader or a chief justice admit he is no more than a front for the chief executive? It's a charade they have to play if for no other reason than to keep their moral up! Could any political gene worth its salt take this ignominy lying down? It doesn't, it fights tooth and nail, with little results but better catharsis than Carter's Little Liver Pills.

Even that super-realist LBJ, as majority leader under Eisenhower, had himself and his ninety-nine colleagues convinced that the country would fall apart without them; but as weak as Ike was, he kept Medicare and a dozen other pieces of legislature frozen right where he wanted them.

And every chief justice from John Marshall on has pontificated on the supremacy of the courts—but over whom? Not over the chief executive. When was the last time they had to make a decision on the presidency, much less affect it. And if RMN didn't show the Justice Department and the courts where they stood via Cox and the tapes, no chief executive ever will.

Even Cal Coolidge and Warren Harding made the Congress and the Courts take high dives, balance on tightropes, and walk the plank. But having vowed to do what is necessary to get reelected so help them God, the Congress goes through its paces like trained seals, filing committee reports, authorizing, debating, pronouncing, appropriating, resolving, and everything else the public show demands, with a great stir of creativity and accomplishment. The president magnanimously throws them an occasional herring for balancing the ball and blowing the horn, but not one anchovy if they balk.

Like Wampum and Hudson Bay

The checkless (and feckless) congressional arm of the system may not work so well, but the legislators are only taking Thomas Jefferson at his word when he said, "The government is best which governs least." It's the greatest spectator sport since Nero's coliseum, and as fixed and routine as Tuesday night's professional wrestling. Besides shuffling papers and putting out their quota of press releases for home consumption, the lawmakers play their own rather exciting in-house games (on both sides of the aisle). They make their own rules, scuffling over scraps of power, choosing leaders and whips, the best committee posts and chairmen by cliques and cabals like any byzantine fiefdom. The success of such energy puts some few in better positions to bargain and trade their votes and power—like wampum or any other nonlegal tender. In season, the Congress is the busiest trading post since Hudson Bay. During LBJ's reign as majority leader, every day was market day and you traded with him or not at all.

As in any big kill, every member of the pack or tribe gets his share. In the Congress, there's something for everyone, whether committees (or commissions) with plenty of staff, worldwide junkets, investigative units with TV privileges, or even a simple hideaway in the Capitol. By their seniority rules, the oldest get the best and the most, which is probably as fair a way as any. Fair or not, and young Turks notwithstanding, it'll stay that way come the Revolution. As long as the wealth is shared, all are relatively preoccupied. If they are not totally happy, they complain little except along approved party lines (which is more or less expected and also helps to liven the show).

Advise and Contend

As Senator Everett Dirksen used to grumble in his gravelly baritone, "The Congress can't start anything, but it can block most everything." To lend a semblance of importance and utility to a senator's life, the scholars invented Advise and Consent. This check on presidential appointments was only given in the spirit of *noblesse oblige*, but no president has ever been happy with it. The power-poor Senate grabbed it and ran. It's been the best bargaining bait (or presidential blackmail) this inert body ever had. They've latched onto it and played it to a fair-the-well. Under the proper circumstances, with the right president in the right year and with a worthwhile trade off, Haynesworth and Carswell would have been a shoo-in. Ringo Starr or Liberace could have made it if the congressional heavens were more placid and the political price was right.

The "consenting" on the new vice presidential nominee after Agnew's resignation was probably the most complicated back-room deal since the fatal merger of the Penn-Central. Mixed up with Watergate and the tapes, the president paid for it in blood (to both parties) and more blue-bearded sweat than he shed in the 1960 TV debates. The Ford in his future may mean the difference between the open road and the prison wall.

The auctioneer for all of this executive-legislative horse trading is the majority leader—especially when the other party is in the White House. However, because of his statesmanlike position as middleman, he has the Senate Whip do the dirty work—the menial bargaining and settling for each and every in-house transaction. (Of course, if it's a deal in his home state, the majority leader takes a direct hand, chancing no slip-ups by his account-keeping bagman.)

The Whip keeps his ledger like St. Peter, chalking up gold stars and black marks on his good or naughty senators and recording what's coming in and going out: bills to be killed and bills to be sold, who to confirm and who to deny. He can make or break any senator by putting off a vote till he can be there, or putting it on when he won't. But whatever he does, he gets his cut, his pound of flesh, a leg up on that majority leadership. Little Bobby Byrd, the right-wing West Virginian senator, stole this job right from under Teddy Kennedy's nose by simply being the best valet to his colleagues' menial needs. No beta rhesus monkey ever did it better in as meticulous a grooming operation as ever seen on Capitol Hill. He saw that each of his colleagues was well laundered and did a little extracurricular shoe-shining on the side while Teddy was sporting on the national scene. In this liberal Democratic Senate this former KKKer will surely be the next majority leader—maintaining the ideologic integrity of that great body.

The One-Room Capitol

Another act that helps convey a public impression of usefulness is Discuss and Debate. The august Senate chambers would be as cobwebbed and musty as a ghost town if the system didn't demand at least a daily matinee with specials (like filibusters and cloture votes) every once in a while to keep the tourists excited. It's old-fashioned vaudeville, which even the participants enjoy. But when it comes right down to it, all that "willful little bunch" needs is a simple little cloakroom out of the public eye, where their business and their wills can be done (fashion did away with the cloaks).

Any self-respecting Capitol architect who doesn't know this simple political fact should go back to planning Parthenons. Nothing happens in open sessions that hasn't been decided in the "cloakroom." As LBJ put it to his team on both sides of the aisle, "Work it all out in the cloakroom. When you're finished, then you can come out and debate a *leetle* [as he was wont to pronounce it when he was wheedling] before you vote."

This great deliberative body, this most exclusive club of one hundred individualists, tolerates every conceivable point of view—except dissent. But even dissension is not beyond the cloakroom pale. The last dissent arose five years ago when Senator Dodd of Connecticut in a unsenatorial way put principle before survival. He insisted that using his campaign funds for personal expenses was not a breach of ethics pointing a shaky finger at the other ninety-nine. He must have been in an advanced stage of senility, for though no one wanted to censure him, he refused a cloakroom compromise.

Prior to this, it had been fifteen years since a Senator (Joe McCarthy) was put up by his peers for detailed public scrutiny. He was duly censured, but it took five years to do it. They are not called "deliberative" for nothing.

This hard-working, selfless group is dedicated to the proposition that no matter what the travail, inconvenience, or hardship, above all else comes the preservation of their good offices and each other—for the common weal. Nowhere is the survival instinct more obvious and effective (Dodd and McCarthy notwithstanding). In a matter of this import (reelection), the aisle is no longer a gulf or a barrier—it's a flower-strewn dance floor. The Democrats and Republicans waltz together and change partners as at a square dance. There are unwritten laws couched in mellifluous phrases embellished with the "honorable senator from here or there," which hides nothing.

When it comes to a situation on that Senate floor that might hurt any one of them back home presidents and partys go out the window and it's all worked out together. Imagine the naïveté of the junior senator from North Carolina putting an antiabortion amendment into the foreign aid bill without consultation and putting every senator on a razor's edge between his Catholic constituency and his Planned Parenters. It was, of course, passed unanimously on the floor (for the Catholics) and has already been virtually killed in conference (for the Planned Parenters), and Senator Helms has learned a lesson in good government.

Nothing takes precedence over *senatorial courtesy*, and woe it is to any of that noble one hundred who dares breach the law of the chambers, bonding or no bonding. No member, no way, at no time, dare condemn or impugn the character or infringe on the prerogative or bailiwick of another of his number, unless the provocation is tantamount to murder and the victim is a senator. Teddy Kennedy's problem was defended and hushed up even by Republicans, for in nonpartisan trying times when the whole body may be impugned, it's *E Pluribus Unum*. Anyway, as an ultra candid congressman from New Jersey put it after Chappaquiddick, "It could have been worse —it could have been me."

One must give senators their due when it comes to national security, war and peace, or the health and welfare of constituents. Their reelection and only their reelection can deflect their interest from these crucial national issues.

The Other (Fifth)—The Greatest Show of Dearth

As to the House—the other half of the legislative branch— according to the time it puts in and the results it accomplishes, it's more like a "fifth." This lower house could literally be labeled the "fifth," for if ever a body needed the kind of stimulation and means to forget, that a *fifth* can give, it's this one.

Representatives are supposedly closer to their constituency

(a situation almost intolerable in itself) and must show up at least every eighteen months to face the music. They themselves feel underprivileged, for as they see it, they are more equal than the Senate but rendered less secure and less prestigious by pure constitutional whim.

The House has been tossed a few meaty bones like initiating money bills through the "Wilbur Mills Committee," but most of their hundreds of committees and subcommittees are for no greater purpose than providing staff and help not allowed by the ordinary budget. The committees may have semimonthly meetings (or more often if there is television coverage), but as that powerful congressman, Mendel Rivers from South Carolina, used to say, "Why waste time meeting if the votes are already counted?"

Speaking of that great Southern American, committees can be useful. Rivers was a master of the committee system and used it as it should be used. As chairman of the Armed Services Committee, he saw to it that if there was ever an attack on the United States, the president and the Congress would have to choose South Carolina over Fort Knox for maximum protection. It had more military installations than the Maginot Line and the Sino-Russian border combined, and the greatest single source of nonfighting military personnel anywhere but in the Pentagon itself.

The Impeachable Sorce

The lower house (so aptly named) has other menial duties. For instance, it devolves on them to start impeachment proceedings (only because the Founding Fathers knew the Senate would have none of it). But in two hundred years, they've only started them against a president once, though they've had dozens of excellent opportunities. It's not done more often for obvious reasons: first, it involves work and attendance (with their three-day work week it could go on forever); and more important, members are fully cognizant of the pitfalls of political life—there but for the grace of God go they. As courageous

Wilbur Mills (a man who got where he is by taking his own advice) said: "Never never get in front of your troops until you're sure the battle is won."

The one time they did bite the bullet, with President Andrew Johnson, it had little to do with ethics, morals, or legality; it had more to do with politics. The discourtesy of the president in not allowing certain congressmen their due windfall in the Reconstruction of the South was just too much to take lying down.

Now they have another crack at showing their mettle as a decisive body, realizing their potential, and (on the side) putting it to their envied rivals, the senators, who make the final decision—all in one shot. They'll muff this one, too. Sure, they got the vice president to swing gently, gently in the breeze, but only by default; the president had laid the groundwork to allow himself a little breather. But they won't touch Nixon until they have their backs to the wall. Which means they'll probably have to wait another eight or twelve years for another shot at a president.

The Congress—"that little group of willful men with no opinion but their own," as President Wilson described it— all in all does the job expected of it. It is usually uncomplaining, keeps a stiff upper lip (a tribute to members' self-control), and continues to put on a show that is as professional as the Rockettes. The public loves it. Some voters would give up television or pro football rather than relinquish the entertainment value of the great congressional extravaganza.

Carved in Jello

The number 3 power in the separation—the judicial branch— is as different from number 2 as number 2 is from number 1. First, it displays little sign of life, much less activity. By contrast to Congress, the Supreme Court justices have a certain suspended animation, like an Iwo Jima statue carved in jello. We know they move, for every once in a while they quiver and announce a decision. They rarely pester the executive branch, but help get the legislative branch off the hook on occasion when they clarify or reject something the lawmakers never quite understood as they voted for it.

In the scheme of things, the Supreme Bench is extremely decorative (though at times ponderously so). Even if this body did less, it would still give one a feeling of solidity, dignity, and even awe. If for no other reason than this, it should be kept around. These nine pillars of justice, usually devoted to the ideology of whatever president chose them, whose only fun in life is clobbering a law some legislative body dreamed up, have only one great fallacy. Members usually outlive the terms of the presidents who could have used them so well, and thus the next administration is often stuck with nine curmudgeons who can't be trusted to do his bidding.

The Executive—Watergate Tells It All

The executive branch needs no further analysis. In government, two words explain it—*all powerful*. Then if everything there is to say hasn't been said by Watergate, it can never be explained. It's all there in print, sound, and living color, an open book that spares precious little detail and relates right back to its source—the jungle. Despite the Congress and the courts, the chief executive goes unchecked (and as it is intimated by the press, unbalanced).

The only other filler in this show of shows—the vice presidency—is expeditiously dispensed with by quoting Ben Franklin's address of this understudy: "Your superfluous excellency." But superfluous or not, even Ford, who as a football star at Michigan had to read his signals from a crib on his Mickey Mouse watch, has a headstart on the big one next time around.

So this is democracy, a system run like any other wolf pack except for the drag of its two subsidiary components, frequently termed poisons and antidotes. These two, if they have any excuse at all, can be used by the executive on occasions as the best possible subterfuge or as a substitute for decision-making. They also, at the least, give the electorate a sense of representative government. In practice, the system seems to be fulfilling not a democratic but an anarchistic hope, in that at least two out of its three arms have withered away, if not died. But the congressional arm will probably never go completely. The indefatigable survival will of individual congressmen and senators is comparable only to that of the cockroach, who will be here long after the nuclear holocaust. From the looks of it, so will they.

XII

The Party of the Third Part

(*Them and Us*)

The demmycratic party ain't on speakin' terms with itself.

. . .

The raypublican party broke ye but now that ye're down we'll not turn a cold shoulder to ye. Come in and we'll keep ye broke.
—Mr. Dooley (Finley Dunne)

Propinquity and assortive mating will greatly increase the number of marriages between those that carry genes for similar aptitudes, *or party voters*. This will not necessarily yield a bumper crop of geniuses, or *Democrats or Republicans*, but it enhances the possibility. [Italics added]
—Theodosius Dobzhansky

The government of a baboon's society is just what it appears to be only because there are no known baboon political scientists (though there are a plethora of political scientists who are baboons). There have been no reports of philosophical simians who conceived of their leader or their rank and file as any better, holier, or more democratic than what they actually were—so there was no reason for governments of the baboon, by the baboon, and for the baboon. Baboon society is still growing and prospering under an executive system of born professionals, without the benefit of a congress or supreme court.

Though baboons are lucky to be free of this burden, they are at the same time deprived of one of the most spectacular extravaganzas ever put on by man. The jockeying, obstructing, and finessing of the three branches of human government as they try to cancel each other out is without doubt the greatest show on earth. But it is entertainment reserved only for the unfortunate human.

The Shadowy Government

Human government is fun but it can't be all show and excitement. As we've mentioned before, the political scientists thought through only how a political system should look and act, not how it should work. And that's why politicians must come in two convenient models. There is the shiny bright, who is elected and put out in front for all to see; and then there is the other nonidentical twin, the party politician who wakes his illustrious brother each morning, winds him up, slips the programming card for the day into the slot, and sends him on his way.

In these modern publicity-conscious times, this more shadowy party of the second part is something of an anachronism, for he operates in politics unsung, unheralded, without stars in his eyes, and without hair-styling, much less tooth-capping. He's the man behind the man behind the system. He is his brother's keeper.

As there were political philosophers and political scientists who could devise outlandish schemes, there are party politicians just as ingenious who can unravel, circumvent, fix, plug, vent, or polish these systems to function. They may reap some minor personal benefits from their labors, but less than they are due. When Secretary of State Paul Powell of Illinois died, they may have found three million dollars stuffed in his shoe boxes, but, after all, he helped run one of the largest states in the Union. As old "pol" Plunkitt of Tammany said when acknowledging his personal gain in politics, "I seen my opportunities and took 'em." After all, they run a   ation.

Party politicians are the salt of the earth,   ut they don't have a particularly good public image because a few of their members, like Kenney or Hague in New Jersey and Carmine DeSapio in New York, were caught. But the   are thousands of smarter, more careful ones, like Jack Pollack and Mimi

DiPietro of Baltimore, Joe Mazolla of San Francisco, Patrick J. "Sonny" McDonough of Boston, and Joe Crangle of New York who are as clean as the driven snow.

They may not have the style and polish of their brothers, but collecting the dues, filling the union halls, printing the sample ballots, manning the phone banks and getting the voters out and paid for doesn't call for black tie. Of course, if they had the front, the bright young Harvard staffers, the Preen Machine parts, and Brooks Brothers tailors, they'd be the suave officials they now elect and serve instead of their keepers.

That fellow with the cigar clamped solidly in his teeth may turn the stomach of an Alice Roosevelt Longworth, but whether she knows it or not, he is the one (not her favorite senatorial dinner partner) who greases the skids and grinds the gears that move the wheels that run the house that Tom—and George—built. He is the fixer between the voter and the winner. He is the one who has the potholes filled, sees that the garbage is collected, and helps bring the aged old grandmother over from the old country.

But in this day and age of imagery even this earthy group needs window dressing. What plausible excuse for those two *leaders* of the National Committees—Robert Strauss and George Bush—who are tailored on Bond Street, banked on Wall Street, and almost acceptable at Georgetown's P Street tables, except to bring the faithful together every four years in one piece. As LBJ said, "Those *Fancy Dans* couldn't cut a deal with a volunteer stamp licker on his first day at party headquarters."

The Pro—Hopefully Not the "Con"

The party pro's language may not be that of a choir boy, but his semantics are rarely misinterpreted; he may be short on democratic philosophy and other esoterica, but he knows there are only two ideologies—*them* and *us*. He may not be able to charm a women's auxilliary at a candle-lit fund-raiser, but he is the life of a stag smoker and a gasser at imitating

FDR and RMN. He may not pick the right fork for salad but he can pick the right candidate to win.

He is not without ego, but he is also not obsessed with acclaim or applause; he is satisfied just to be seen stepping out of his "man's" Continental as he leaves him off at the neighborhood tavern. At times, he may have to become completely self-effacing, taking off "on little cats feet" for the more salubrious (if anonymous and less confining) climes of Mexico or Honduras until things blow over.

This worthy is generous (near election time), loyal (to his meal ticket), and compassionate to the downtrodden (with large voting families). He could cut a deal with a Persian carpet salesman, compromise with a Uzbek diplomat, or be tough and as mean as a Korean bodyguard. He wears no Roman collar, but is closer to the parishioners than their confessor, knows more about family problems and finances and the going rate of "vigorish" than the friendly loan shark, and in time of trouble is called long before the lawyer or the bondsman. He may be a younger breed today but he's still bibulous, bellied, bountiful, and puts nothing in writing. The likes of John Lindsay he isn't, but he's our man in government, and he is good at it.

These diamonds in the rough, who have been so maligned, impugned, and belabored in print and cartoon from Samuel Johnson's and Hogarth's day to that of von Hoffman and Herblock, live up to every bit of their reputation—but that's government. They are down-to-earth and know that precincts aren't stolen and elections won without warm bodies, hot shoe leather, tough minds, and lots of money. As to the last, they may be closer to Mammon than to God, and though they're generally religious, in their experience the lord of lucre seems to produce better than the more spiritual one.

Somehow, when one thinks of party politicians, it's difficult to come up with even a single Republican of note. With Democrats, it's easy: New York's great Boss Tweed, Boston's renowned Curley, Chicago's monarchial Daley, and FDR's Jim Farley. The only one in recent Republican history who distinguished himself (other than Daugherty, who whelped and warped Warren Harding in the twenties) was John Mitchell, who would have been better off remaining anonymous. But then again, why should Republicans have to bother with party chiefs? They can bide their time and count on the suicidal conversion of the Democratic majority (about thirty million if all were registered) from party to principle every eight years or so, when they give their all to "sweet charity" and the Republicans.

Two Ideologies—Them and Us

County Chairmen, ward bosses, machine regulars, and precinct leaders are like congressmen—indestructable. Though neither learned in anthropology nor cognizant of Darwin, they have more survival savvy than a barrel of baboons. Imagine what it took for the Republican party indestructibles to come back from their bloody licking after the Goldwater debacle in '64 and get it all back in '68. If the Democrats return from the grave of '72, it will be as miraculous as the arising on Easter morn or as lucky as Watergate. But win, lose, or draw, the pols pick themselves up off the barroom floor the day after the votes are counted, and like their little worker ant cousins, busily go back to milking their aphids, tending their tiny fungi, and getting *us* ready for *them* again.

They are the complete pragmatists. They know their way may not be godly, nor even legal but they're doing the best they can with what those learned scholars handed them. They patiently give a full hearing to all those theoretical eggheads who couldn't tell a poll watcher from a polecat or a smoke-filled room from a bright golden haze on the meadow, and though they've heard it bruited around that ideology is just peachy, they don't let it bog them down.

It's not that the party politician doesn't think big or want man to express his highest aspirations, but at election time the teats of the pro are as dry of the milk of ideologic kindness as the withered dugs of a menopausal witch. They just can't be worried about mankind and *them* too—not and win at the same time. They're concerned about the important things like "walking-around money," precinct runners, poll watchers, and whether their counterpart in the next ward will cut their own man from the ticket and most of all who's doing the counting. As the notorious Tweed once said, "I don't care who votes as long as I'm counting."

There are only two ideologies to the political pro—them and us. It all began with one iota of species difference: The spots of the leopard signalize alarm to the tiger, as the stripes of the tiger are a red light to the water buffalo. Each is afraid of the other, only because he's different. The starlings close ranks with just a glimpse of the deadly falcon; hackles go up as the wolves and the deers catch just a whiff of each other (like the automatic twitch of the Cabot or Lodge nostril when accidentally caught in a South Boston Democrat's ward). No matter whether it's the animal or political jungle, there is always a "them" and an "us."

Our modern party system is a living example of the party pro bringing "hackle raising" up to civilized levels. He cleverly puts to work all of the simple survival mechanisms—security, excitement, identity, and especially xenophobia—all without having read a single book on cultural psychology. But it comes easy for him, for he dates back to the early *Homo erectus* politician, the first one to up the ante, setting the precedent of majority rule—winner take all, including a crack at posterity. His successor after him, the brainy Stone Age man, then formed the clan and tribe and did what all good parties try to do —killed off all the others. He must have been a huge success, for no other less brainy human is here to tell the tale. Then, as is the wont of civilized man and the modern politician, they did a little long division on "them and us" and came up with political parties, like all successful synagogues, churchs, or PTAs do. Reading Kevin Phillips it is clear that the mechanics of ethnic voting is fueled with hatred and with envy.

Over a couple of thousand years, the party politician eventually made xenophobia a game of the people, labeled it Republican, Democrat, Populist, or what have you, and began collecting dues. At last almost everyone had something to fight for or be suspicious of, or be linked to: color of skin, slant of eyes, brand of religion, quirk of brain, length of hair, or any combination thereof. In a stroke of political acumen, these were all put together in one wastebasket called *Ideology*. It was only then that special interests, bigots, snobs, and illiterates of any faction could admit they hated blacks, were against the draft, welfare, eggheads, or long hair; or for the SST, trusts, low taxes, and high interest, without saying so. It was a political idea whose day was long overdue and it was the making of the modern political party.

Political pros like Jim Farley and Larry O'Brien, without reading Leakey, Dart, or Margaret Mead, took this kind of basic "we and them" anthropology and made it into a thing of beauty and a joy forever. It simply required organizing those differences to get them on the smooth macadamed road to the White House rather than the garden path to the outhouse.

The Politics of Togetherness

At rock bottom it's all just a matter of genetics and demography. It's who they are, who they came from, and where they're crowded together in the brand new science called population genetics (in which every good politician is a professor emeritus). Harry Truman explained it all in five words: "Parties are born, not made." Obviously, if parties are born, so are Democrats and Republicans.

In other words, we get back to those "peas in a pod," the tiny little devils that make politicians and followers, and thus parties—Democrats, Republicans, and Independents.

To put it simply, those who pray, play, and lay together will stay together—and vote together. And so will their mothers and their cousins and their aunts. For instance, a Polish UAW member in good standing in Detroit, having always gone to his neighborhood church and school, will more likely be attracted to a Polish foreman's daughter down the street than he would to a French countess or a Sardinian shepherdess. Not only because they have more in common, but she's there and he doesn't have to travel three thousand miles or swim the Atlantic Ocean to meet her. After a hundred generations their offspring will not only look, eat, and think alike, they'll also vote for the same party.

The party pols aren't up on Dobzhansky's theories of genetic pools, but they know why they can deliver solidly in Bedford-Stuyvesant or Cook County. They know that those born with more compassion, have a greater feel for the underdog, youth, peace marchers, welfare mothers, featherbedders, and generally giving the sucker a break: The Democratic party can count on them on election day. It can't however account for such phenomena as more votes being cast for Johnson and Kennedy in some precincts in 1960 in Texas than there were voters.

On the other hand, the political eyeball geneticists can spot the less idealistic, more conservative, Establishment kind, who are repelled by welfare, Jerry Rubin (and who isn't?), Arthur Schlesinger, and Ralph Nadar's activists, and write them off to the Republicans.

The Blindfold Test

Any politician worth his salt can pass the political blindfold test. He can tell a Democrat from a Republican at twenty paces. As LBJ put it, "My pappy warned me, if you can't come into a room full of strangers and tell who is for you and who is against you [Democrat, Republican, or Kook] get out of politics." To put it simply, just one glance or three words with them is enough. Try to picture Ambassador Henry Cabot Lodge or former Attorney General Elliot Richardson as populist Democrats, or Abe Beame or Arthur Goldberg as Goldwater Republicans.

Even the maverick Independent is a genetic lot that can be spotted a mile away. Dissident, nonconforming, they come out squealing and kicking even against the middle they were born to. Their only claim in politics is spoiling. It was a toss-up whether they would vote for Gene McCarthy or comedian Pat Paulsen in the 1968 presidential election. Though the parties make a cursory pass at them, it's a reflex; there are enough who come down on either side, usually, to cancel each other out.

Bella and Strom—Mission Impossible

There are also pools within pools. A voter isn't just white or black, he's also Catholic or Jewish, bright or stupid, educated or uneducated, and speaks like a Bostonian or a Georgian. He's the net result of a combination of traits. For better or worse, as with the Polish auto worker, the more bad habits a male and female have in common, the more likely they are to meet, mate, and produce replicas of themselves.

For instance, the chance that Bella Abzug as a white (not-so-nice) liberal Jewish girl living in New York would be thrown in, much less have an affair with, a white weight-lifting, jogging Protestant Conservative like Strom Thurmond from way down in South Carolina is, to say the least, far-fetched (though they both work for the same company). Three out of four of their pool characteristics are way out of kilter. With Shirley Chisholm and George Wallace, it's four out of four, or possibly ten out of ten, but here only one would do the trick.

Ideologic repulsion alone (which is more than skin-deep) should keep Ronald Reagan from lusting after the physically attractive Gloria Steinem, or a Louise Day Hicks from falling for Teddy Kennedy.

It's "everything we always suspected about politics but were afraid to ask." Likes attract likes and produce like personalities that will pick their parents' political party for the same reasons their parents did. It's nothing new. It's just like the inborn national characteristics of the efficient German, the excitable Italian, the lyrical, boozy Irishman (wherever they're born) who prefer Wagner, Puccini, and the "wild Irish rose"—as each suited their special personalities best—and always will.

Of course, the Skinner bunch will still stick to Pavlov: Condition a voter to be a Republican and that he'll be. If so, about fifty million Italian, Irish, and Jews in America didn't salivate right when the bell rang. These three gene pools fifty years ago were supposedly drawn to the Democratic party because it was the party of the minority, the poor, the downtrodden. But now, rich and assimilated into the highest strata of society, they are, strangely, still Democrats. Catholics, though no longer of minority status, should be Republican, but still persist in voting Democratic. The Midwest farm bloc is as Republican as it was in the 1800s, regardless of Democratic price supports, land banks, and the beating it took from the Republicans on the Russian wheat deal.

The Forgotten Tit

Today, the New Left, the New Politics, the reformers, Fred Harris' New Populists, and Shirley MacLaine notwithstanding, the party pros are not withering. Coincidentally the National Committees have fallen on hard times and are calling for help from the pros, who would like nothing more than to see the expendable expended. That party facade in the Capitol may become as extinct as the deep-sea coelacanth. After Watergate blew the Republican party cover, it became obvious that the National Committee has been a prehistoric fish all along. It was overdue for extinction. All it ever did was bleed the grass roots for the hot house orchids. LBJ in 1963 said, "It's seen its better days and is about as useful as the hind tit on a boar." Marshal McLuhan put it in a little less homey way: "The party system is folding like the old organizational chart. Policies and issues are useless. The shaping of a candidate's image has taken the place of conflicting points of view."

But who needs a million-dollar (a-year) boar's tit? If there was one that showed the parties up for what they weren't, it was the Republican National Committee in 1972. They were the forgotten boar's tit of the 1972 campaign when CREEP, the greatest little money-raiser the Republicans ever dug up, took over.

In 1963, just before his death, John Kennedy brought the Irish mafia together and laid it on the line "don't bother with the DNC, the '64 campaign will be run from the White House."

LBJ, who saw the handwriting on the wall, did with intent for the Democrats what John Mitchell did by accident for the

Republicans—he threw the first shovelful on the National Committee's grave. Old Sam Rayburn had taught LBJ a lesson he never forgot when he lost the first time in his run for the Senate: "If the party in Washington can't help you in your district, don't let it hurt you." Johnson took old Sam's advice in 1964. He "stomped it out." Show the boar's tit as its own useless self was what HHH did—almost winning without one. And party or no party, it was a rare Democrat up for election in 1972 who didn't hide behind the barn when he saw George coming (and poor-mouthed the party treasury).

Today the National Committee for the Democrats is less a fund-raising machine than a debtor's prison. Of the Republicans—the less said, the better. And if there was a time when all good men should have come to the aid of their party, they didn't—neither party, in 1968 or in 1972.

Even though Bobby Kennedy's two million in arrears was added to the party debt in 1968, Teddy hardly turned a hair. Between conventions Muskie, McGovern, and Scoop Jackson (the candidate troika) were just as hard to get out on the stump, but when they did finally come, they demanded a lion's share of the gate plus expenses. This kind of dyed-in-the-wool loyalty can only be matched by George McGovern, who at one time refused his money list to the very party that nominated him.

If Teddy Kennedy goes in 1976 with his already growing organization of old faithfuls and his own access to money (it's a rare politician, who uses his own, even the Kennedys), he'll give Strauss' debt-ridden setup as wide a berth as Richard Nixon gave the national GOP in 1972.

Though it may now have passed its peak, the National Committee did once fill a need. It gave employment to hundreds of the mentally handicapped and unemployables, keeping undesirables off the streets and away from the racetracks, giving succor to losing politicians and a place for them to lick their wounds and maybe even try again. There were planks and platforms and issues to give a little lift and entertainment to a convention. And certainly a convention has to be organized and contracts drawn. We know now that all of this could be done better by a business manager with an adding machine, a mimeograph, and a computer. (Welfare now takes care of the downtrodden, regardless of party affiliation.)

Republicans 1972—In the Finest Party Tradition

The *coup de grace* to *both* grand old parties was Watergate. The Committee to Reelect had its usual mundane political purposes, but its remarkable innovations bordered on the genius (imagine laundering money in the Rio Grande).

In concept, as glimpsed at the Senate hearings, it was a marvel of American efficiency: using the tops in political shakedown artists (Secretary of Commerce Stans, presidential lawyer Kalmbach and even columnist Safire); a system of in and out revolving bank accounts that would give David Rockefeller vertigo; the dirtiest of dirty tricksters (imagine linking HHH with loose women); fake telegrams, asking for IRS collusion, and a quota system for the 100 top corporations that had never been dreamed of before by the willy nilly nickel and dime Democrats. It was pure twenty-first century Tweed—a glimpse of the future.

But in execution it was cops and robberish which not only gave the whole national pastime a bad name and a death blow to fund raising for 1974—but was a black eye for every pro in the business. Besides it did the unpardonable—it got caught. Even Jess Unruh a pro among pros who said "money is the mother's milk of politics and I've sucked every teat in town" never tried to swallow the nipple whole.

What got the American voter really riled up and mortally wounded the National Committee was not the deception, the petty skimming, the burglaries, or even the cover-up. These are taken for granted. It was two things: first, the political *gaucherie* of such a non-professional and utterly useless caper; and, more important, that their good money was going to *common thieves* rather than *common politicians*. Though some of it supposedly went for good causes like the San Clemente and Key Biscayne White Houses (four million of which seems to be still revolving), the constituents just can't forgive their favorite political charity for hiring other burglars to do their job for them. As Mencken said, "The plain people are not hostile to shysterism save it be gross and unsuccessful."

To top it off, the noisy do-gooders, the new politicians, the league of women sanitizers, added fuel to the fire, stirring up the sleeping voters even more. From their big-mouthed example, the voter now has the gall to question where political funds are coming from and whom they are going to. It's a sad state of affairs after two hundred years of building a fund-hiding maze of dead ends, red herrings, and blind alleys (all of which J. Edgar Hoover would have had trouble tracking), that now the American voter has lost faith in the tried-and-true party methods.

Thus the rumors of the impending death of the national committees are not exaggerated. For there is a spate of election reform bills in Congress that would have party politics run like a super-market—keeping the Committee middlemen from skimming the cream. Over this the ubiquitous machine pros will shed no tears.

But if Congress, the National Committees, their chairmen, and the Mr. Cleans think ward and precinct leaders will dry up and blow away in this political self-immolation, they'd better consult their Tarot cards again. The local pros will not only use the new congressional system of payoff, but will also become the legitimate custodians of the *common wealth* (in keeping with the present fad for decentralization) and they'll spread it out so well it will take the GAO, the FBI, the CIA, and the Hawaii-Five-O to figure it out—if they ever do. Their Washington big brothers may stay and wither, or go and good riddance, but the professional—never!

Geno-Politics

Other than high political finance, there is a new day dawning for the adaptable machine pro. He's going to have to prove himself at least as endurable as a baboon or a congressman. Up until now, he's had that little old-fashioned political abacus clicking away in his head, weighing, balancing, and summing up all the genetic pros and cons and coming up with who is for him and who is against him. And he hasn't done half-bad.

Just as he's coped with reformers who made it difficult for the political enthusiast to vote more than once or prevented the faithful from casting "the last one" for a buried uncle, and even as he put up with the new voting machines, so he'll roll with the scientific punch and eventually use it for the good of his party.

Eyeballing is out. The new discovery of the double helix, which programs every cell in the body and the body as a whole, especially programs politicians. The diagnosis of the political DNA will not only help rid politics of the National Committees, but will also do in the political Nostradamuses.

As explained in a previous chapter, with one cell from a fetus we will be able (in the not too distant future) to determine whether the yet-born will be a politician. And by teasing the information from those same chromosomes and using a little of the new population genetics, we can get a fix on the party that that bundle of cells will be attracted to at age eighteen in 1992.

Then, by feeding a little more living information to the punch card, the computer will take into account every inherited or acquired bias, bent, or influence possible. It can't miss! In thirty seconds, it'll come up with the exact candidate an Italo-American voter from Providence, Rhode Island, age twenty-five, who spent six months in the priesthood (quitting to marry an Irish waitress in his father's restaurant), graduated from Fordham (flunking female studies), and is making twelve thousand a year (but reporting only nine) will choose in a presidential race in 1988. Here, political meteorology, a subject in itself, comes into its own—the shifting of political climates by the changes in the winds and tides of population shift and growth. (It was mainly this changed climate, not a newly enlightened southern liberalism that put black Charles Evers in as Mayor of Fayetteville, Mississippi. It was also the climate, not the Greening of America that put Catholic JFK in where Al Smith lost. The increase in the number of Catholics from twenty million in 1928 to forty million in 1960 [the total population had only risen by a third] played a big part in his slim victory).

By tagging every infant at birth, the new science of geno-politics, using the gene, demography, population genetics, and the computer, will make gubernatorial races a snap and put congressional contests in the back pocket of every boss who can buy the print-out (or rent a computer)—as long as he gets just the right genes to the polls on time. It could have saved fifty million dollars for Adlai Stevenson, Humphrey, and McGovern—just by telling them ahead of time, "Slim or no chance"; it could have saved all that newsprint, those straw hats, buttons, anguish, and energy. It could also prevent ten thousand U.S. megalomaniacs from wasting their time running for councilmen, mayor, or what have you. It could announce winners as soon as a hat is thrown into the ring, months before a lever is pulled.

However this new New Politics would deliver one great blow to a great American institution—the leather-lunged, haranguing, interminable, righteously indignant citizen mass meetings, and their devotees. Those deprived but energetic thousands who look forward to this kind of sadomasochistic exercise will have to take up karate or some other means to vent their spleen.

As to the orthodox political scientist, he would have little to do but work out unlikely academic puzzles on the probable party affiliation of the progeny of a poor Puerto Rican Catholic living in Kansas City married to a wealthy Anglo-American Episcopalian from Mississippi.

Technology will bring the physician, scientist, and computer into the world of politics. And the holy-rolling of the academic political pundits will take its rightful place in history beside the blood-letting barber surgeons. The primitive polling of Harris and Scammon will be looked back on nostalgically and fondly, as we now do on the *Hagerstown Almanac*.

The National Committee will consist of only one little technical wizard in a lone room on Capitol Hill surrounded by up-to-date tapes of every birth in every precinct in the country. But he will only be a keeper and advisor. It'll still be the party pro down in the wards and precincts with his own little staff of scientists and his leased computer who'll call the shots.

But as long as the scientists, physicians, and technicians are of flesh and blood, even their computer would get an offer it couldn't refuse and at least some of the warm, human, everyday corruption of party politics may be salvaged.

XIII

Lusting for the Hustings

(A *Psycho-Sexual Endurance Contest*)

It's as beautiful and simple as all great swindles.
—O'HENRY

The campaign for a public office is allegedly to *educate* the electorate to a candidate's view and to *expose* his character, strength, and ability so that the voters may choose the best. In spirit, it is a Christian endeavor not unlike the Crusades; practically, it is an exercise in obfuscation so that the truth will never see the light of day. No known politician could expose himself to this kind of scrutiny and still win. So he sees his course and he takes it.

A campaign is like a game to test the voter's acumen. In the spirit of self-preservation, the candidate and his team must camouflage, obscure, or cover each and every blemish of mind, soul, and character. It's up to the voter to pierce the disguise and flush him out. The voter loses either way, for even the lesser of two evils is no great boon to the democratic process. No wonder "In God we trust."

Lust, Not Titillation

The philosophy of campaigns, of course, has little to do with the necessity for them. The politician girds for the campaign trail as automatically as the salesman anticipates his route, the

pilot his wild blue yonder, and the salmon her trails, tribulations, and pleasures as she wends her way to her spawning
grounds two thousand miles away. The animal wanderlust still
lingers in the human blood. For the politician, it's much more
than just the excitement of travel or the titillations of faraway
places. It is the instinct of the migratory bird, coupled with
the lust of Genghis Khan plus the everyday thrills of the road
and the Crusader's spirit, as they killed and conquered to save
the world.

What greater fun than battling, plundering, and gorging one
night in a desert town, the next in a mountain village; the
camaraderie on the trail, the boozing and wenching—all for a
good cause? Every bit of this ancient lust is caught in the political campaign. As the time approaches the candidate tastes it
on his buds and detects it in his nostrils and drools in anticipa-
tion.

Though the politician's life is always mobile, at campaign
time he is the complete nomad. It fulfills his every need, reviving his job security as he basks in a new and wider identity
and recognition. It releases him from boredom as it renews his
bonding and gives him the thrill of the chase at the same time.
After the relative orderly routines of political (and marital) life
in his own territory, the politician itches for the uncertainty,
the gamble, and especially the freedom of campaign chaos.

Chaotic Discipline

Prehistoric man's treks across the tundras of the world
couldn't have been as chaotic and disorganized as even the
best-disciplined campaign. If they had been, the Stone Age
would still be with us. But looking at those equally low-browed
chinless teams attracted to campaigns (not exactly Neanderthal,
but neither entirely Sapien) who chart the course of the political expedition, it's a wonder it has survived as an institution.

How could these microcephalic types ever hope to coordinate
financing, logistics, local issues, speeches, press releases, and
a dozen other incidentals, while planing, deplaning, motorcad-
ing, crossing, and recrossing a state or a nation. This is the stuff

for sophisticated logistical, financial, and management experts. But there has been no campaign to date that could ever lure one in—not after he took one good look at it; and if he did take the bait he would no doubt be entangled, suffocated, and buried in the morass his first day on duty.

As Ralph Dungan, one of JFK's top organization men, said (in a supposedly well-organized—or as he said, well-disguised—campaign), there was never a day passed in 1960 that they all didn't sigh three Hail Marys each time their man got to the right podium in the right city on approximately the same day, with the right speech and the correct release, without some foul-up that the press might see and report.

Once in the 1972 California primary, Hubert Humphrey's plane and pilot refused to budge because the crew had not been paid in three weeks. In 1952, Estes Kefauver's campaign aides wound up in one city and he in another. In 1972, Eunice Shriver was programmed at a huge Baltimore Bull Roast where her microphone was cut off, she was spattered with salad (tossed), and just about bodily ejected (who'd ever eject Eunice?) in a minor campaign fiasco—it was a Democrats for Nixon rally.

One would think that after two hundred years of the process of electing leaders in our representative form of government, there would be an accumulative wisdom, or a system, or at least some guidelines for an orderly campaign. Even the most retarded rat will run a maze successfully after trying it fifty or so times. But not so with election campaigns.

However, how could it be different if there is no campaign manager (or candidate) yet known whose memory stretches over more than four years? Attesting to this is the fact that few of them ever run more than one successful campaign. The day after the election is like the day after electric shock therapy —the brain is wiped as clean as a slate. This is true for both winner and loser, and for different reasons: the winner because of his euphoria, the loser because of his depression. Neither of them want to be reminded of a six-month nightmare that must have accelerated the aging process at least as much as a high cholesterol diet and a spendthrift mistress combined.

The Diagnosis—Campaign Fever; The Cure—None

The stirring of campaign fever in Washington is like the pre–Civil War malaria epidemics that swept the city. First, one is bitten by the infected bug (which has a taste for legal blood), then the lingering disease blossoms to maturity on or about October before the third November after the previous presidential election. There are then vague stirrings, a restlessness, some minor hallucinatory delusions and anticipations, with difficulty in concentrating on normal work.

There is then an acceleration of metabolism up to convention time, with loss of appetite (except sexual). Only alcohol as the nutritional staple helps assuage the fever (if not the fervor). Then follows the postconvention defervesence; by August, there is a monomaniacal fixed stare to the eyes, an amnesia for family and home, and a compulsion to speak in unintelligible phrases understood only by sick people like themselves. The fever pitch climaxes and ends in early November. The patient then gets much worse, with severe depressions, nausea, and malaise lasting for months (for which there is no quick cure), or he wakes up one morning and is temporarily completely well and maybe feels even better than before he was bitten.

This, of course, is not the same brand of the illness that attacks the candidate. The candidate's is more chronic, congenital, and almost entirely cerebral. It may be alleviated, but like schizophrenia, it usually recurs. Study the case histories of Napoleon, Churchill, LBJ, or JFK—the syndrome is there from swaddling clothes to shroud.

The symptoms are classic. In the candidate's dream-like state (or delirium), he awakens with "Ruffles and Flourishes" and switches on the *Today* show after a restless night (always in Lincoln's bed). With barely half an eye open, he salivates as he vicariously sees himself making the News of the World, which brings to mind *Meet the Press* and how he must call Larry Spivak for a date. As he shaves, the bristley presidential bust morosely stares back at him, surrounded by the usual semicircle of stars (even before the first primary) as his stream-of-consciousness reminds him that the UAW's Woodcock hasn't called or contributed, that his campaign needs some vehicles, that they still owe the airlines from the last campaign, and how he'll get a contribution from the lobbyist he's having breakfast with at the Mayflower.

A quick cup of coffee and a dash of cream before leaving reminds him that the Milk Cooperative hasn't come through with their bit and a radio commercial has him humming and rhyming a new campaign jingle. He kisses his wife goodbye, wondering why she's still in curlers and not at an early coffee klatch.

Otherwise, his mind remains uncluttered and free for the duties for which he was elected. His first call from the hotel to his Senate office tells him his schedule for the day, the votes that will be coming up, and that the majority whip is mad as hell because he missed three quorum calls yesterday. This wraps up his congressional business for the day. (It was estimated that there were weeks when all four top presidential candidates in the 1972 primaries spent maybe two hours apiece, if that much, in the Capitol.)

The candidate then begins his real day by calling his campaign manager. The phone rings ten times before it's picked up and a foggy voice, as in a comatose state, answers. He reminds his manager of at least a dozen calls he must make, an idea for a fund-raiser, that a cousin of his wants to work in the Washington headquarters, and to get that SOB off his back who almost ruined him in the last campaign and insists that he has the one and only strategy to win with—this time.

The Anatomy of a Campaign Manager

The campaign manager curses those early-morning calls, barely listens in his general amnesic state, and promptly forgets everything the candidate says in the welter of the daily new demands, complaints, and reminders.

A nephew of Adlai Stevenson's was supposed to have been hired to cover a district in California in 1956 and it wasn't until election day that Stevenson found out he was never called. Hubert Humphrey ordered that Norman Cousins be asked to write a draft of his September 30 Vietnam plea to the nation—

the call was never made. John Y. Brown (of Kentucky Fried Chicken), one of the best fund raisers in the business, was forgotten in a slight oversight after he volunteered his services to a debt-ridden presidential candidate.

Campaign managers are either hacks or amateurs, and since the hacks never learn by experience, they might as well be amateurs. They are usually dredged up from one of the fifteen thousand or so Washington attorneys who come down with the four-year itch. They are all equally choosy. The foremost criterion is that the candidate's family is more or less behind him; the second is whether he can afford to at least set up an office; the third is that he, the aspiring manager, doesn't have to contribute to the rent or make a loan of his car. Other trivia like the candidate's ideology, principles, and program can always be worked out later.

The manager's credentials may include a college thesis on some inconsequential aspect of a long-forgotten campaign, a civil liberties speech prepared for a freshman congressman, or (most important) a close friendship with the candidate's brother-in-law. He may not be entirely convinced, but is convincing that he can lead the candidate to the White House. However, if for some reason the candidate (or his brother-in-law) can't see his way clear to grab him up and thus be assured of the presidency, he would accept an advance man's job in Delaware or Rhode Island.

For some reason, lawyers abound in this dubious field, and after some of the dubious lawyers who abounded in Watergate, it's understandable that their legal knowledge must not only give them confidence, but also come in pretty handy in avoiding nasty little postcampaign sequelae in the good fellowship of investigating committees. They also seem to meet every test of emotional instability, mental torpor, and physical lassitude. Humphrey's Bill Connell was about as placid as a blue tailed fly. Muskie's general staff Bernhardt, English, et al. (except Mark Shields—a political natural depressed by his grand motherly client who took to his beer with ice cubes [and bourbon chaser] early on to save his balance if not his candidate) seemed intellectually aroused only by fancy restaurants.

The campaign manager's intellectual astuteness has to be at least one notch above the candidate's—which is about as minimal as one can get—but more important, he must have a feel for candidate husbandry. Here John Mitchell may have fallen a little short on the first count, but was admirable on the second.

Short, Sweet, and Very Low

The professional life of the campaign impressario is short-lived, almost like the fleeting existence of the May fly—one shot and he's finished. However, he will pop up in some capacity henceforth and evermore. Political graveyards are full of these unknown soldiers. For every one of the unusual ones such as Jim Farley (he also came to a premature end), there are hundreds who couldn't come out for the last round.

Larry O'Brien, touted as the pro of them all, had his big fling in 1960 and lived off its memories (and a postmaster general's annuity), recycled himself in 1968 but was side-tracked in Bobby's campaign, latched onto HHH and lost, and came to an ignominious end by his own hand and McGovern's help in his "peace in our time" convention in 1972. Campaign managers don't last long enough even to pass their own expertise along —and maybe that's a good thing.

John Mitchell, another success story with Nixon in 1968, should have quit when he was ahead. Any campaign manager who doesn't realize that bugging a National Committee chairman's office is an exercise in sterility is either a fool or was lucky the first time. On his judgment alone he should be isolated for his own safe keeping.

Frank Mankiewicz's impeccable credentials included his family's illustrious name in political movie-making (*Citizen Kane*), a dry run for an office in California, and the dubious credit that he got along with the press. Even this extensive political background didn't give him any greater longevity than most others. He had been around the track a few times in Class B roles till he managed to euchre himself into the top-banana spot with the embryonic McGovern campaign. After elbowing

his way through Gordon Weil and Gary Hart to the top of
that shaky ladder, he skillfully convinced the press that Mc-
Govern won the primaries. He then proceeded to take it all
apart by inciting the HHH people in California, sneering at
Muskie's campaign, denying Daley a seat in Miami, riling
George Meany to a white-hot rage, and then engineering the
biggest bummer decision of all times—the Eagleton affair with
the 1,000 percent statement. To top it all off, he put Larry
O'Brien out to pasture. LBJ, after the Miami Convention,
said that this sometimes hero to the New Left (before he
alienated the women and the blacks) could "fuck up a wet
dream."

Regardless of Race, Creed, or Ideology

There are a host of other political dilittantes who manage
candidates switching from liberal to conservative and back again,
as the pressures demand (any port in a storm). Hy Raskin and
Ben Wattenberg, for example, the shopworn ADAers with
conservative Scoop Jackson as a candidate. Many of these
managers are put in by close "friends" of the candidate to be
sure the "friends" have control not only of the candidate, but
also of the campaign.

Among the rankest amateurs was HHH's pure Minnesota
cornball, Jack Chestnut, an ideologic neuter, a converted advance man who could rarely be found except alone in bed (with
little to say when he was) and a financial genius in borrowing
from Peter to pay Paul. In the end Humphrey was left with a
campaign debt his children will have to work off by washing
dishes for AT&T or American Airlines for the rest of their days.

Then there was Dick Aurelio (John Lindsay's man), running
a national primary campaign when he had never been south
or west of Lincoln Tunnel.

Muskie had a mixed bag of amateurs, run-of-the-mill legal
minds, and a sprinkling of political hacks. Early on, he had
every national bandwagon jumper known, from Clark Clifford
to Jim Loeb. This combined management expertise took him
from frontrunner to tailback in three short months.

Headhunters Anonymous

The inner campaign maneuvering among the staff may be more predacious and cannibalistic than a paranoid headhunting tribe. Traveling by its instincts, the campaign family's hunger for human flesh is such that if they aren't sinking their teeth into the opposition, it's into their own kith and kin. Frequently, the in-fighting never comes to light, except that one notices many faces that started in the campaign are missing on election day (especially a losing one), and they are usually never seen again—unless someone opens the proverbial closet.

There is no such thing as a happy campaign "organization" and the history of their ups and downs has as many versions as there are campaign chiefs. Each of the McGovern honchos has written his own account of that debacle, and according to those who've read the books they must have all been in different campaigns.

In every campaign, everyone anywhere near the top thinks he can do it better. In 1972, the McGovern camp became Slaughterhouse-One. The gutters ran with amateur blood, which not only gladdened the hearts of every three-a-week columnist on the trail (practically all McGovernites), but completely overshadowed every issue the candidate ever brought out (as if any of them could have saved him).

Watergate, in turn, brought out the abiding trust and benignity of the Nixon campaign forces; but only when it was all over. These vampires—who came out only after the sun had set (on them)—not only wanted the blood, but the arteries and veins that went with it. Though there hasn't been much book writing from these insiders (which most of them will automatically become), it has more than been made up for in the testimony already given.

The salivating on the lower rungs for the tinier spoils of prestige, position, and even a little cash (as John Dean demonstrated), becomes tinged with blood as it progresses, especially with a candidate who looks like a winner. For where one stands when the campaign ends says where one sits when high office begins. This is how a campaign differs from the ordinary hankerings of early man. They only ate each other in the lean days when their pickings were slim.

At every echelon, from the candidate's valet and advance man to the Jim Rowe level of senior advisor, advice keeps pouring into the number 1 ear, always with a little poison for the others. McGovern's ear was as available to political dilettante Shirley MacLaine as it was to political expert Fred Dutton. Frequently, personal vendettas over an idea, a judgment, or a stewardess can make the difference between winning and losing. The candidate, whose life is on the line, is only semiconscious of what goes on around him.

This is not to say that the candidate is taken for granted, especially his physical well-being. There is a standing rule; a candidate's scheduled appearance is only canceled if there is a total mental collapse or cardiac failure. The candidate's nutrition is scheduled in the carefully planned drug counter stops somewhere on the motorcade route. His excretory functions can always be put off a day or so and his exercise and recreation are worked in by brisk walks to and from the podium. His sexual needs are mainly attended to vicariously, in fantasy, or in the knowledge that this is the main leisure, and frequently working, preoccupation of his staff.

The Wizard of Bite and Other Campaign Fauna

After the manager, the other top advisors are chosen with equal circumspection from the athletes and show biz decorations to the makeup man. The finance chairman is picked in the most businesslike way: carefully weighing his personal contributions, the income of his friends and family, the notes he is willing to sign, and the promises extracted for more to come.

Without these "bite" wizards there is no campaign. Maurice Stans, former Secretary of Commerce, will probably go down as one of the best of all times. He took Jess Unruh's advice literally, "if you can't milk the big contributors, eat their food, and kick them in the ass, you don't belong in politics." He was able to raise money from airlines and milk cooperatives so painlessly that even in court few remembered they'd contributed. He was also the innovator who brought the foreign Laundromat into politics to wash and iron money. To this day, Senator Ervin's committee doesn't know for sure whether Nixon campaign funds were ever touched by human hands. As a former banker, Stans obviously didn't trust his own, for stashed cash seemed to pop up in every White House safe, coffee tin, and it's said even in Lincoln's bed's mattress. By contrast, one old-fashioned fund raiser, who handled money for Kennedy, Johnson, and Humphrey conveniently forgot who and what it was for.

The issues people are predominantly refugees from the Brookings (type) Institution who have rarely indulged in real life. A campaign is their only opportunity to creep out from under the academic rock and brighten their drab lives. They'll do anything (for free) just to be listened to. The part they all secretly look forward to is their one trip on the campaign plane to get the flavor and sentiment. From all appearances, it seems the flavor is ethyl and the sentiment is sexual.

The candidates sometimes read their erudite papers and memos and may on occasion take them seriously. (George McGovern's one-thousand-dollars-a-year to every citizen was an academic's brainchild; it almost cost him the nomination, and killed him completely in the campaign.) But what they have to say on taxes, war, and trade is usually only used as speech fillers, unless one of them comes up with an unusually catchy phrase like "no taxation without representation."

Tripping—Campaign Style

More important than these routine campaign fixtures are the logistics and moving parts of the traveling circus. For instance, one of the crucial early decisions is the choice of airline. The criteria are strict and again businesslike. First, how much the airline contributes and is willing to gamble on a winning candidate. (In hard times an airline can go broke with a loser.) The credit allowed is also important, for banks are not too trusting until after a winning election. Probably third, and possibly second in priority, way above the safety record of the line, is the caliber of the stewardesses—marital status, availability, vulnerability, entertainment value, special functional proclivities, and talents. Whether they can serve a cup of coffee without scalding the candidate on a bad-weather hop is also taken into consideration.

The closest thing to the standard of living of even the cheapest campaign would be either that of Louis XIV or Henry VIII—except for the candidate (he lives well but is so busy, so guarded, and so preoccupied, he doesn't even know how his other half lives). Waste is a way of life. Every one of these high livers in the traveling party, from the advance man to the baggage checker, who are ordinarily at home on a daily fare of hamburger, chuck roast, and fried chicken, with a can of beer and Thursday nights at Gino's, become instant connoisseurs of Châteaubriand on flaming swords (summarily returned to the kitchen if not of exactly the right temperature), Château Mouton Rothschild 1949 (chilled), their morning eggs Benedict, and snacks at odd hours. It's first-class airfare, taxis, and suites all the way. It wouldn't enter their minds that just cutting the fat could put the candidate on network prime time for at least an hour.

But it's the palace guard who set the tone. Room service is *de rigueur*, not only to set an example and keep up their prestige, but also because some of their confidential associations would never hold up in a public dining room nor in a police court. This upper crust, the strategists who stay back in a camp while the candidate is out doing battle, have a Churchillian concept, in that most of their best work is done in bed (their brains seem to work better when not drained of their blood supply by the upright position). However, when they are ambulatory—beginning at about 3 P.M.—they are a vision in motion, if not in accomplishment.

The press secretary's position in his capacity of handling the Fourth Estate (or the *animals*, as they're endearingly referred to) is probably as critical as any. He is privy to all the strategy, campaign secrets, gambits, and new issues. He must be *au courant* with all of these inner secrets to make sure the press's luggage doesn't go astray, that their booze supply is ample and varied (according to individual tastes), that they are awakened on time to catch the motorcade, and that their hangovers are well attended and treated. Also in keeping with his specialized training, he does a magnificent job in handing out mimeographed press releases with a resounding "no comment" after. Getting an occasional reporter an exclusive interview with the candidate is a feat. The networks, *Time*, *Newsweek*, the *Post*, and the *Times* get them quicker than he can —on their own. On rare occasions, he is quoted as an authoritative source, which pleases him no end.

Other than the problem of keeping staff from giving quotable quotes that get the candidate in trouble, one of the press secretary's toughest jobs is keeping each petty chief from trying to get written about. The campaign manager is always the worst offender. The criterion of a first-rate campaign manager is one who gets less press than the candidate.

A whole campaign may hinge solely on how well these duties are carried out. Pierre Salinger did such a great job in his nursemaiding that JFK could have come out for euthanasia, war with Italy, Israel, and Ireland, and a tax on pregnancy and he would have gotten good press. Norman Sherman—HHH's fun-loving press secretary in 1968—almost lost Texas for the candidate when he answered a call from LBJ with "Lyndon who?"

Scheduling for a Wake

Scheduling takes the judgment, timing, and objectivity of a skilled surgeon and maybe that's why so many of the operations are a failure. But with a little luck, some of the candidates survive. It's not easy to sift through five hundred requests a week and have to choose among the AFL-CIO, the B'nai B'rith, and the Royal Hibernians, all vying for the candidate on the same night. Personal preferences and blunders, however, usually overcome even the little good judgment around.

One female scheduler in a presidential campaign almost turned down an American Legion Convention in Milwaukee for a fashion show at the Waldorf. Adlai Stevenson supposedly wound up by some good planning in the same restaurant in Chicago where the Mafia was holding an important meeting, and had the local police, the FBI, and the CIA stakeout in a state of hysteria until he left. Willkie was deftly scheduled into a hotel where he had to cross labor picket lines, and George Wallace, it's said, came close to attending an NAACP convention.

Jack Kennedy used to tell of the skilled scheduling by Ken O'Donnell of a navy yard which was shut tight the Saturday morning his entourage of staff and newsmen got there. He managed to talk his way past the Irish watchman, and as a member of a Senate Maritime Subcommittee, went down to inspect a sub (anything so as not to let the press know what a staff foulup it was), and with his luck, it was one of the new nuclear subs. It put him on the front page of every newspaper in the country.

It's said that Estes Kefauver, by a scheduling mixup, wound up at a Republican meeting, his speech all prepared, and didn't know it until he was almost on the podium.

The Hustlers

The advance operation that prepares for the candidate's visit is truly a Neanderthal band, which is even ordered to live off the land, the party, and the natives. They're like the scouts in a chimpanzee troop, hooting and hollering in advance for their chief. Usually this breed is from the clan of bored lawyers who love the itinerant life and enjoy the adulation they get by misrepresenting themselves to the locals as either a candidate's boyhood friend or a frequent visitor to the Oval Office. They live in a grand style on promises the candidate himself wouldn't dare make. After one campaign, if they have that special something (a combination of snake oil, used-car, and discount-house salesmanship), they would be well prepared to argue and win any type of case up to and including those before the Supreme Court. This talent earns its spurs by the size of the crowd it can drum up, if not by its success at bribing the police chief to raise his crowd estimate for the morning paper. Crowds are for no purpose except to convince reporters that the masses are wild for the candidate—it can be composed of denizens of the local kindergarten, road gangs, wetbacks, or mental defectives (none of whom can vote)—as long as it's big and noisy.

Another important duty the advance has is seeing to it that

the motorcade has no hitches: it must miss rush-hour traffic, not forget to pick up the mayor and the congressman from the district, and—though this may sound ridiculous—not forget the candidate himself. It's important to be at the right place at least sometime before the crowd goes home.

The highly-touted epitome of this aboriginal breed is Jerry Bruno, who wrote a book elevating these nonesuches almost to the level of howling monkeys. He has made the most of nothing. He was even given a professorship for his expertise of trucking in field hands for JFK's political rallies (with a minimum wage of a pint of Sauterne, a boozy day in the city, and a plastic straw hat to sport). For Bobby, Bruno worked out a more sophisticated gambit. He had the bishop of every diocese in the country well oiled with a Kennedy promise of untold aid and succor to the Faith, in exchange for a parochial school holiday on the "day of the candidate," with the girls trained in squealing and tearing off cuff links and other parts of his apparel.

A Sure-Fire Test

There are many other bits of practical campaign lore and technique too numerous to mention or too lurid for belief. But as true of many other aspects of politics, a campaign needn't fulfill a real need. If it educates and convinces anyone of anything, it's that it is the most hardy of all the perennial, if fraudulent, displays demanded by the great American electorate. If it proves anything at all, it's that a fool loves to be fooled and the fooler loves doing it—and a small fortune can be spent in the process.

But it's a universal, not just an American phenomenon. It takes on the coloration of the specific locale as with guns in Latin America, stilletoes in Italy, and stilted prose in England. Nothing could have brought it to a halt but the Communist Manifesto and the one party system. But this could be reversed if the public had its way—it might just be the thing that brings down the whole Soviet shebang.

But it does fulfill the instinctual wander-and-conquer lust of the politician and the public's need to have a recurrent phantasmagoric release with bands, crowds, and emotion-elevating, if not consciousness raising, sessions.

The political results are rarely influenced by either the substance or calibre of the campaign. The run-of-the-mill brain and spirit will still be elected. But if nothing else, it is a sure-fire test of the physical and psychosexual fiber of the ones who are to hold high office—which, after all, is no small thing.

XIV

Convention-al Mayhem

(*The Call of the Wild*)

There is something about national conventions as fascinating as a revival or a hanging.

—H. L. MENCKEN

Few will quarrel with the propositions that overcrowding has a profound effect on human behavior. Experimentally, as crowding increases in a rat colony, an animal nightmare grows developing into a violent, hypersexual, bisexual, and frequently cannibalistic *behavioral sink* (as Dr. Calhoun at The National Institute of Mental Health termed it).

—ROBERT ARDREY

Political conventions are "behavioral sinks" as surely as an overpopulated experimental rat colony. As if by design, convention crowding initiates the same violence, aggression, defiance of authority, sexual excesses, and cannibalistic tendencies; the only difference is that the rats don't go voluntarily. Politicians not only enjoy conventions, but will beg, borrow, promise, and steal to get to one even though it's hazardous to their health. For staying behind hurts worse; it's hazardous to their pride, prestige, and power. (The purge of the pros from the 1972 Democratic Convention did more for Nixon than ITT, Howard Hughes, and the Milk Cooperatives combined.)

The national political convention satisfied every lust the politician is heir to—political and otherwise—even more so than a campaign. For under "one roof" in a convention city, he gets the security of the mob, the excitement of the chase, and most of all, every bit of recognition, identification, and hero worship he can absorb in a period of one week. But more, it's the finest and readiest milieu to incite to riot. What else was Teddy Roosevelt demanding when he thundered at the 1916 convention "To you who have come here to spend and be spent in the endless crusade against wrong I say to you: 'We stand at Armageddon and battle for the Lord.'"

It is also exhilarating to those dominating alpha genes, for the only game in sight in Convention City is *domination*. Of the 5 percent of all human creatures with a dominant gene, most of them wind up at one time or another at a political convention.

Like the Smell of Blood

Even amidst the manners, mores, debaucheries, and strange costumes of the rank and file in their quadrennial package deal (a week in Jungle City without inhibitions), dominance is the theme. But a deeper, and a darker, hidden impulse that wells up from within the ancient political marrow is the real motivation—aggression. The very thought of a convention to a politician is like the smell of blood to a killer shark, the sight of a tender rabbit to a hungry fox, or the touch of satiny young breasts to an aging lecher.

To the uninitiated, the political convention city may look as jolly and prankish as an American Legion jamboree, but to the pro it's about as Fun City as Buchenwald. There is serious business at hand—power business—and it is as deadly as it comes. For the national political conventions are fraught with more political booby traps, ambushes, and caches of explosives (with short fuses sputtering all over the place) than a Weatherman's monthly social. It is no place for the faint of heart. The baths, the salt air, and the fleshpots are there only to refresh and revive the troops and enable them to finish out the *longest week*.

He Tries It—He Likes It

But political aggression is not all bad. Though it may end in political suicide, murder, and carnivorous excesses, those are only by-products of the basic motive, which is—survival. The

aggressive instinct is programmed into the gene only to bring
the potential of that gene to its ultimate. In practically everything, but in politics especially, aggression is only a healthy
(or unhealthy) competitiveness to show who is boss. Though
he may take it to extremes, the aggressive candidate isn't necessarily vicious. It's only that he has spent months and years
showing that he is better in larger and larger ways and this is
the end of the trail. All Fun City signifies is that he has
roamed beyond his own bailiwick, cased the territory, decided
he likes it, and has made up his mind that he wants it—all. If
it's in him, he is there to show that his fangs are longer and
his will is stronger than the rest and that he can make off
with the carcass.

This may be a little too simplistic. The Nobel laureate Konrad
Lorenz has pointed out that "crowding is the root of all mal-
functions of human social behavior." Why, then, should such
a naturally malfunctioning subspecies as *Politicus Americanus*
look for more of the same? Well, for one thing, it may be
just the natural instincts being freed—the call of the wild. The
political animal wasn't always cooped up as he is now in his
state or district, having to act out the prim and proper charade
that is expected of him. It's like releasing a leopard or a
chimpanzee from the confines of a zoo. Only at the convention
can the politician strip himself to the buff, with no surprise
to anyone, even his constituents (as Ardrey says, no one likes
violence more than the spectator), and streak it, blemishes and
all. And the buff shall set them free.

Conventional Sodom

Has the significance of the time and place of political conventions ever occurred to students of politics? It is always in the
incubatorlike tropical heat of July or August, stimulating to
the most primitive of senses: the swarming, mating, and aggressive urges. Could one imagine anything more cloying to
the political sensitivity or the aggressive bent than a convention
in Duluth, Minnesota, in January? All energies would perforce
be consumed in warming the blood or braving the drifts.

The Boston ward heeler and the delegate from Dubuque

salivate over the prospects of Atlantic City or Miami Beach, but not for their health-giving natural resources. The closest a delegate comes to the beach is the sand in his Spanish soufflé, and if the tang of the ocean reaches his nostrils, it's as he savors his red snapper *en papillote*.

The real clue to the aggression leitmotif in political conventions is that Chicago is the perennial favorite of the faithful. This mecca, of all others in America, bespeaks the added psychological dimension of a history rich in aggression, with the classic St. Valentine's Day Massacre as a reminder. Even the smell and the sight of the stockyards is a release to the political predator. It just feels good to the twitching snout, the glowing retina, and the pricked ear.

The overall perspective and life-giving energy of a convention reminds one of the queen termite and her swarm as described by Eugene Marais in his classic on the "white ant":

> The whole behavior of the termite is determined by the invisible influence from the organism of the queen alone, deep in the royal chamber of the termitary. When swarming, "thousands upon thousands of these sexually mature insects fill the air drifting for a few days like a cloud of smoke darkening the atmosphere."

Convention City seems no less a termitary in full swing. Any national convention city soon takes on the looks, sounds, and smells of the convention. After twenty-four hours, everyone gyrates and reverberates like Ping-Pong balls in a wind tunnel. The jostling bodies, heaving and swaying crowds, and bumper-to-bumper traffic with straw hats, stickers, pamphlets, buttons, and beauties in a wheeling kaleidoscope is the crowding conducive to the battle they all seek. From the volunteer to the candidate, the cacophony of clattering helicopters, roaring boats and cars, the rattle of dishes punctuated by the relative quiet of shouting caucuses, and the boozy wee-hour screams of the chasings through lobby and corridor is a symphony to their ears.

Not only do sights and sounds usher in the future president of a nation, but also an all-pervading convention odor. No

Grasse *parfumer* could ever duplicate the mélange of aromas that hangs like smog over Convention City. They all seem to merge in the waiting queues inside the velvet ropes of the *maître d*. The subtle combination of alcoholic perspiration, sun-tan lotion, pizza, and My Sin all mix with the smell of broiling sirloin. Though it may have felled more than one wheezing beer-bellied asthmatic politician, it's as stimulating to the average delegate as a bagful of uppers.

As Lorenz says, "With concentrations of people, aggression gets out of hand." The physical and mental trials and tribulations of a political convention may be the final test. Jim Farley described it in the 1932 nomination of Roosevelt: "I was near the point of mental and physical exhaustion and conducted the rest of business that night with Senators, bosses, Vice Presidential candidates, and even Sam Rayburn from a cot in the tiny gallery headquarters."

It's as if convening is for the purpose of weeding out. John Kennedy may have had Addison's disease, "Ike" Eisenhower ileitis and a coronary, and LBJ a coronary and kidney and gallbladder stones, but by surviving the convention physically—and winning in this "out of hand" milieu—they proved they could take it mentally as well.

Although convention excesses in the short run are debilitating and depleting (and the lower in the hierarchy, the more this is true), in the long run they are renewing and reviving for the average politician. If he survives them, there is little doubt that after a month or so of convalescence (preferably in an intensive-care unit), the therapy of release carries him over for four more years. It is said to be superior to purging and bloodletting, and at least as good for the soul as confession.

The Art of the Impossible

Political conventions are the times that try men's roles. For the principals, it is a battle to the death—mastadons with locked tusks contesting for power. For the pack, it's the excitement of contending with its rivals for a kill. The outward behavior at conventions—the girding, preening, wallowing, wolfing, grooming, baring, and bristling—is like all other animal contests:

just the surface show to the preternatural will to dominate. Even the sexual feats (retold on cold wintery nights in the the warm, beery taverns in Newark) are only part of the power show. But the human doesn't stop at show. Aggression gets out of hand—or "jumps the tracks," as Lorenz stated it. It comes down to a knuckle-dusting, no-holds-barred battle that the Marquis of Queensbury would shudder to contemplate. The candidate leads as hungry and mean a group of predators as any Hun or Tartar band and they are ready, willing, and able to use all of the primitive tribal ploys to make their kill—the nomination.

Old Boss Crump of Tennessee used to grumble, "Rules are for after you get elected." There may be honor among thieves, but at political conventions, honor goeth before the greed. As aggression accelerates, rules and ethics go down the drain. A political gentleman is only a gentleman after he has won, and a handshake is a greeting not a covenant.

From the royal chamber of the king bee, as Marais said, "the invisible influence stems" and the top aides are as antsy as any drone doing its fidgety dance to show it has scented nectar. Their telephonic antennae are buzzing, minute by minute probing, wangling, dangling, and wrapping up over and over, even with their own delegation, much less just a shaky one.

It's playback and replay, assuring and being reassured that things are the way they were yesterday or ten minutes ago. A front-runner beginning to slide may be deep in the mud while the pats and plaudits are still warm on his back and ringing in his ears.

The royal chamber gets a blow-by-blow body count from the so-called *boiler room*—the ready room—down below where every delegate is marked blue, red, or yellow—for, against, or maybe. And like a battle chart, the shifting tides are watched by the high command and orders to retreat, reinforce, or attack may change in a matter of hours. There are the "whips" of every candidate in every delegation who telephone their big boiler room agents three times a day. This agent, with his handy little household dossier on each delegate's tastes, weaknesses, deprivations, and financial problems, gives the order: "Hold hands, promise wives, wine, dine, and cater to the delegate's every whim" in the best interest of the candidate and the democratic process. Tickets, reservations, and party invitations for the delegate's mothers, wives, and aunts are there to grease the skids. Coercion, cajolery, threats, bribery, and seduction are the means at hand. Bobby Kennedy promised a private audience with the Pope to a delegate leader in New Jersey, and in the same convention in 1960 LBJ assured two senators his majority leadership. Jim Farley, in 1932, knew the first name of the wives of practically every Texas delegate. FDR needed Texas badly and John Nance Garner's gift of the vice presidency finally sewed it up.

Every erg of power is used. If there is a sudden change of heart, red lights flash in the boiler room and the big guns are brought to bear. An alert could precipitate anything from upping the ante to a direct call to the stubborn delegate's boss from the "man" himself.

Apple Pie and Unfixed Conventions

Now, though it may sound un-American, only a fixed convention produces a president. The bitter battles nominating Goldwater in 1964, Humphrey in 1968, and McGovern in 1972 nominated losers. Only those smooth, well-orchestrated symphonies of Ike in 1956, JFK in 1960, and Nixon in 1968 produced sure-fire winners.

Even so, as in any auction or crap game (and a convention is a bit of both), anything can happen. Though most of what is on display has been "knocked down and locked up" way back, each delegation is open to offers, especially on the second, third, or ninth ballot. Though the game may be fixed, it can become unfixed.

All delegations, no matter how nailed down, became a medium of exchange when the price is right. This price fluctuates with the daily fortunes of a candidate, as if on the floor of the Exchange. The going rates rise and fall with rumor, releases, and announcements of support. A delegation one day may be worth three assistant secretaries, a missile site, with two (Latin American) ambassadorships thrown in; and the next day, it may be down to one assistant in the Small Business

Administration. For instance, a front-runner like John Kennedy in 1960 could get part of a delegation for just one U.S. attorney, or a whole delegation of small states for one Navy yard and three Justice Department appointments.

But up until now, it's been a very hit-and-miss proposition with no real trading center or quotations one can depend upon. This has led many political traders to demand a ticker-tape arrangement in the 1976 Convention that will keep them up to the minute on the current quotations.

A few small, shrewd delegations, which have been offered little and can't expect much and are at or near the right position (the point where a certain candidate could go over the top), may gamble and go uncommitted until the last minute. They'll bargain as long as they can, but though they don't have much to lose, there's always a little something, and it's impossible to catch a bandwagon once it's past. There is no emptier feeling than to be left holding an empty political bag.

Even so, the delegate caucus is in the best tradition of the democratic process. It is a means for each delegate, representative of his people to assert his integrity and political judgment, as long as this doesn't interfere with the deal by which he has been consigned, sealed, and paid for. An occasional representative of the people in the nominating process may live dangerously and make his own deal. He is more likely to die rather than live by this sword.

If an alpha ever has to show his genes, it's in the relatively rare caucus revolutions. As in a wolf pack, if the alpha weakens, the group members begin tearing each other apart until little is left.

Caucuses grumble about having to assemble for an hour or so a day (which takes them away from their fun and their daytime recuperation), but they do have some basic social and educational functions. They give special groups—female, ethnic, and labor organizations—something to get together for, a forum where they can get their petty grievances against each other off their chests. They are also good testing grounds for the party youth and academics. Here they can see how things work in the real world and even learn that occasionally tides do change and it's important to have fire drills for jumping on and off bandwagons. But most of all, they indoctrinate delegates to the basic political proposition that all rubber stamps are created equal and must stay that way. Boss Hague echoed this in his memorable put down of a double crosser, "An honest politician is one [who] when bought—stays bought."

The Big Brass Ring

In this combined auction-room and roulette ambience, as the political calliope blares its steamy tunes and the carousel revolves, the greatest delegation-getter of them all, the big brass ring, is that great afterthought of our constitutional forefathers, the vice presidency. Every mayor, governor, or congressman (even Walter Cronkite was considered by McGovern) who controls a piece of a delegation peddles himself around. This marketing gimmick—this much demeaned office that John Nance Garner (FDR's first vice president) said "isn't worth a bucket of warm spit"—is eyed, savored, and campaigned for as if it were worth something (and it was to Spiro—in large white envelopes). Actually, it is important—one way or the other. It was an *open sesame* for Lyndon Johnson, but walking the plank for Hubert Humphrey.

The vice presidency is played with fast and loose by the giver, but for keeps by the aspirant who must show enough "tooth and nail" and convention support. The vice presidency is worth entire delegations, and in this very common market, it could be valued beyond the combined worth of several cabinet level posts—John Connally was first appointed secretary of the navy in 1960 as a medium of this exchange. Bobby Kennedy had the vice presidency traded to a minimum of four governors and five senators and when JFK chose Lyndon Johnson, Bobby had to hole up for a week. But as JFK explained his choice of the best man to be one heart beat away, if elected he couldn't live with Johnson as majority leader and he could easily control Mansfield (the next in line), and what is more, he needed Texas' electoral votes. He was right on all three counts.

When Humphrey was nominated in 1968 and chose Ed Muskie for his VP, Governor McKiethen of Louisiana, who wanted it so bad he even had bumper stickers made, went over to Nixon the day after. In September of 1968, the disappointed Governor Connally of Texas got himself thoroughly lost (and never was found), he was so busy soliciting his friends' contributions to RMN. (HHH campaigned in that great state a minimum of six times, and only once, two days before the election when Humphrey looked like a winner, did Connally show, at the Astrodome.) Even Senator Fred Harris, Humphrey's campaign co-chairman, went from an active member of the team to a dropout in his vice presidential letdown.

The Sound and the Fury—Conventional Foreplay

All these back-room, barroom, and bathroom (strangely enough, a favorite place for bargaining) maneuverings sort out everything in readiness for the public show. Meanwhile, back at the ranch, on the floor of the convention, there is the sideshow for the viewing public. This entertainment is so arranged for the first few days only for orientation and the dissipation of the rank and file. Until "Wednesday" of "the week," convention hall is "amateur night."

This breather is readily given over to the dilettantes and the idealogues so they can indulge themselves with self-catharsis and be done with and out of the way by the time the real business is at hand. They're allowed (within limits) to keep the action going on credentials, planks, and platforms. They are encouraged (to a point) to liven things up with delegation-seating objections and keynote and "man who" speeches— mostly for appearance's sake. It's good for troop morale and gives the boys in the back room proper cover for their more delicate operations of drawing up the big-night scenario.

It also gives each candidate time to work in some mob-fighting exercise, to and from shoring up some of the more important but shaky caucuses, a few TV shows, a dozen or two of the hundreds of the private parties given by assorted parasites, symbiots, lobbyists, assorted hanger-ons and the omnipresent Washington socialite patriots down "to take the waters." It also gives him time to butter up the convention chairman who can make or break him. JFK found this out in 1956 when several delegations raised hell trying to switch to him but somehow just couldn't catch chairman Sam Rayburn's eye.

Occasionally, these droning preliminaries are enlivened by an outbreak neither in the political scenario nor in the carefully worked out TV programming. For instance, Bella Abzug shook up the planners and brought dozing delegates to their feet at Miami when she suddenly rumbled over chairs and bodies like a Sherman tank (heading for the camera with the best Neilsen rating), her chubby fist flailing, her straw hat askew, thundering, "McGovern sold us down the river. I won't let you bastards get away with this."

The Embroiled Imbroglio

If there is aggression in the political foreplay, well, as Lorenz says, "The tighter men or animals are packed, the more lethal they get." Fun City becomes a drained ghost town as all of its energy is funneled into the sardine-tight arena on *"der nacht."* Even without the old-fashioned, faked-up, paid-for demonstrations, bands, chants, release of balloons, and pigeons, it's an unimaginable nightmare. It's a combined greased-pig and mud-wrestling contest with some of the panic of a raid on a house of ill repute and a dash of the high dives in the Crash of '29. It is *morbus politicus* in all of its glory.

The floor is a boiling sea of delegates, "whips" with their walkie-talkies, row captains, section bosses, and regional chiefs —all in constant motion with a wary eye on one another and a direct line to the boiler room. To worsen the imbroglio, there is the usual hyperkinetic mob of college journalists, home-town reporters, and assorted news freaks who have managed to cadge a badge and add to the confusion; plus a mixed bag of celebrities like John Wayne, Shirley MacLaine, and Norman Mailer wondering in the crush, ready for an interview at the drop of a camera.

Rumors are floated, bandwagons begun, broken down, and started up as if it were all spontaneous. A few cute tricks might be launched such as the calculated South Carolina loss early on by the McGovern forces in 1972 to lull the moderates to think that the California hassle was theirs. But these are rare.

Just as Cronkite Planned It

Added to this is the show-biz network crew, with back pack and camera as aggressive as any politician—not for a vote, but for a Nielsen rating. To the Cronkites and the Brinkleys, it's just their seven o'clock news show expanded to carnival proportions. They are determined that Mr. and Mrs. America will see the political convention only as they program it, and it's interpreted, jazzed up, or toned down as the anchor man in his rafter eyrie sees it—mainly to entertain, but also to factually report during slack periods. The chair and the podium are occasionally panned so that the temporary chairpersons and other political adventurers can get their licks in for the folks back home. And if a candidate or campaign manager thwarts these electronic czars, he's only asking for convention coventry (the silent world of *newspaper only*). None of the networks forgave poor McGovern for being so inept as to give his acceptance speech around 3 A.M.

When CBS or ABC are ready, the droning of the state-by-state polls begin, each advertising themselves and their natural resources: "Mr. Chairman, the oleaginous state of Alaska, land of the walrus, the polar bear, and an equal number of voters casts one-half vote for its own favorite son, the man who made our pipeline possible, and six large votes for four more years." "Mr. Chairman, the great bourbon and blue grass state of Kentucky—the land of former VP Alben Barkley, casts one vote for George McGovern, three for George Wallace, and twenty-seven votes for that 'horse who,' Secretariat." Then there is either wild cheering or booing as it goes from Alaska to Wyoming, which occasions repeating, adding up, and recounting.

In this great nominating game, even a small state that can finesse it to push the winner over the top always rates a warm spot and a little *quo* to boot (JFK never forgot Wyoming in the 1960 convention, as he also never forgot West Virginia for pushing him to the nomination after he beat HHH in the primary there). So they jockey around, passing and relinquishing, watching and waiting to see how the winds from the back room blows. As it gets closer, managers are screaming at delegation leaders, delegates are grabbing microphones, and in the last minute swirl of their *danse macabre* a last hysterical fling occurs as if at a ball in St. Elizabeth's. Then it's over. Losing candidates concede, then winners and losers recede, both toasting themselves stuporous either in a happy delirium or, as Agnew would term it, in a deadly dolorous doldrum.

Hangover Morn and Exodus

In the hazy aftermath of hangover morn, as in the body-strewn aftermath of a battle scene, the vice president is chosen with all due consideration of picking a charwoman. It is said that Goldwater chose Miller while still in bed; JFK had to run LBJ down in a locked unmade hotel room; HHH decided on Muskie in the bathroom; and God knows what Nixon was doing when he chose Spiro.

But even before this happens, before the acceptance speech and before the vice presidential nominating exercise are suffered, the losers are already in exodus. The lame, the halt, and the utterly pickled are carted off on stretchers, wheels, and wings in the first phase of retreat—their hostilities assuaged. When the winners can no longer hold out in their boozy bastions and have all pointed their blue bottoms up in allegiance to the new dominant, they, too, are shipped home depleted and once more docile. Convention City hangs empty and suspended like a deserted wasp's nest. The Super Bowl then shapes up—the dye is cast.

XV

Forgive Him for He Knows Not ...

(The Trizophrenic Politician—a Louse Divided)

As the brain becomes more complex with evolution, . . . we become more vulnerable to emotions.

—Dr. Donald Hebb

If man could understand himself he might not destroy himself.

—Professor Francis Schmitt, M.I.T.

So stands the politician in all of his splendor on the steps of the Capitol, framed by the dome, surrounded by his admiring constituents, being photographed for the high school year book—his best profile toward the camera. Well-tailored, cool and confident, with an air of purpose and performance, he appears the epitome of modern *Homo sapiens*. If history is to be made, he'll make it; if the human is to evolve into something better, he'll lead the way. And he has convinced himself that what made it all possible is that big new brain of his, that organ that separates him from the animal (and also from those admiring constituents).

Brains It Ain't

But something doesn't jibe in that scene. From a distance, it's like a campaign poster, but close up, it ain't necessarily so. Especially the brain part. For of all the different kinds of new human brains—philosophical, artistic, religious, scientific, bureaucratic, and others—it's only the political one that doesn't come off so well. To be perfectly candid, of the various new brain talents, the political brain is well to this side of retardation.

194

How else can the logic, actions, and eccentricities of the politician be explained?

For instance, the philosophical brain has been good at things like determining the number of angels that can dance on the head of a pin—things it's fit for. The scientific one took itself to the moon and back, and even the ordinary brain has shown snatches of brilliance—building Disneyland, writing *Hamlet*, concocting *bernaise* sauce, and inventing the *bidet*. Even the religious brain thought up and successfully merchandized the Immaculate Conception—which was no lead-pipe cinch.

By contrast, the political brain, which could only have gotten into this impossible business by default (there were no other takers), at its very best could only come up with a few mediocre ideas like democracy and the UN. They both sound great but neither measures up. Not only that, but in the political brain's day-to-day dealngs with its own creation, such as laws, agencies, or commissions, it gets poor marks. And it seems to be getting worse, not better.

Now, though the lack of the intellectual wherewithal is a problem of considerable proportions to the politician and his art, it's as nothing compared to his real brain troubles. As Henry Kissinger said, "Who needs intelligence in politics?" But that big, beautiful specimen on the Capitol steps—prancing, preening, and intoning as he shows his best profile—spends most of his time covering up his well-deserved inferiority complex. However, even more disturbing to his peace of mind, crucial to his performance, and jarring to his pride are those embarrassing old instincts as he champs at the bit to be out on crisp fall evenings, baying at the full moon, following a scent, or, like his simian cousin leader, governing without all of the claptrap of laws, statutes, and a hostile electorate.

The Sign of Cain—Long in the Tooth

To all but the trained eye, the politician passes. But as he stands on the steps and smiles for the folks back home, there are some niggling little hints that lets the baboon out of the bag. First, he is just a mite too long in the canines—they protrude a bit over his lower lip. Then up under the jaws are those faint pinkish markings reminiscent of the gill splits of the shark. Neither of these is a reassuring sign. Another less frightening, if rather demeaning, one is a most peculiar wriggling beneath the rear flaps of his vented jacket that might be a well-concealed, if fidgety, prehensile tail.

"Ontogeny recapitulates philogeny" is a phrase learned by heart in every biology class. It simply means that every human embryo in the womb goes through the stages of amoeba, to fish, to monkey, to become a full-fledged human at birth. This is as true for the politician as for the bull frog. Frequently we'll see throwbacks in ordinary humans who have webbed toes and totally hairy bodies. Somehow, they don't occasion a raised eyebrow. But it's something else for that fine-figured leader of men, topped by the big brain (the organ that brought us out of the wilderness), to have retained, of all things, the sign of the shark and the saber-tooth. Perhaps we'd feel much easier if instead he'd been left with the ears of a rabbit or the wattles of a chicken.

None of this would bother us except that the politician is not just a garage mechanic or another corporate executive. He may think what he will of himself and go his egomaniacal way, but wherever he goes, he takes us with him—up or down. So we'd better worry when we see those Bible-quoting paragons sprouting tooth and claw, for in evolution, whether of copperhead, cougar, or politician, a species keeps only the traits it must use. The vestigial signs we see in the county executive do not give us the sense of peace and tranquility we hope for.

A Brain Divided

So besides the usual intellectual underachievement of the politician (which is only too well documented in history), there is that primordial bent that he tries so hard to stuff back in and hide. But it's not easy. Within that political cranium, there is a house divided against itself. As Abraham Lincoln said, it cannot stand, and from the looks of things, it won't. It's being torn up by one of the coldest wars in the history of braindom.

Dr. Paul McLean at the National Institute of Mental

Health, in studying this phenomenon in animals and ordinary humans, has shown that the new, handsome, young gray matter, the cortex—with its active frontal lobes, impressive deep convolutions, and fresh, sparkling snyapses—makes man act in the human way, reading, writing, and having ideas. But it doesn't get a free ride. Lower down, there are two underling leftovers from man's yesteryears that just won't go away.

So there are really three brains in all. The oldest McLean calls the reptilian, and the next oldest the old mammalian brain. These two combined are the instinctual brain, which functions according to ancestral experience, tending to make men act just like snakes, wolves, or baboons would. It not only embarrasses, it gives the cool, urbane, political cortex a fit.

The two brains, the reptilian and the old mammalian, together seem to be concerned mainly with territory, sex, hunting, and even with selecting leaders (as we've shown before, it's instinct not intellect that has to do with political success). It also has the job of protecting itself and preserving the species by its emotions.

But here's where the rub comes in. The newest overlay in the brain—the human one—is supposed to control the other two, or at least oversee the working arrangements among them. Though the instincts go along with this control most of the time, they refuse to be intimidated and especially made a scapegoat for every flub the cortex gets caught in. And the instincts have a good case, for though they interconnect with the cortex, brain-wave studies show they are also independent.

Now if this isn't problem enough for any mortal, think what it does for the decision-making politicians with their limited ability to cope. Judging from political behavior, the old and the new brains may be talking to one another, but not so you could notice it. That house divided will intellectualize on the principle of peace—and bomb everything in sight to prove it.

The Generation Gap

Unlike the newly elected politicians whose troubles are with the old guard, it isn't the old-timers that won't cooperate here —it's the new brain that's impossible to work with.

It's the old story of youth and age, impulsiveness and stability, new ideas and old experiences—a yawning generation gap. Here is this upstart, the new human political brain, only two million years old at most, listening to neither advice nor warning from those two cagey old graybeards. The reptilian and old mammalian brains are not only a couple of billion years the cortex's senior, but are steeped in their own instinctual politics. Who does this new political organ think brought evolution along so far—in fact, to whom does it owe its own existence? Those two wise old heads have more knowledge and experience tucked away in their little medullas than that whole blanket of buzzing new cortical gray matter. Even the scientist and philosopher will ask counsel of these elders—but not the political upstart.

Picasso, Grandma Moses, Tchaikovsky, and Gershwin were not loath to take what the old brain could offer and even plagiarize a bit from cave paintings or jungle rhythms, but the political brain is either too proud or too arrogant to ask for help, even as it goes down for the third time.

Territory: A Means to an End—Everybody's

Take the territorial imperative for instance: a sure political way to peace, spontaneous and carefully matured for eons; good enough for every species from the minnow to the mandrill; saving life, limb, and species. The new human political cortex should have grabbed this idea, had it any sense at all. Even the simple follower brain took it—lock, stock, and barrel. But again, not the politician. He changed it to his way of thinking, converted it into a sure-fire troublemaker with the best lethal potential.

A rattler wouldn't think of attacking another rattler for something it wants. Nor does even the rattler brain dream up principles to stand on, face to lose, or dignity to injure, giving him every excuse to punch his neighbor senseless because of them. The old instinctual brain may not have a new idea every minute like the new cortex, but neither has it conjured up ideologies that sink ships or exterminate cities. Together, the lower reptilian and the old mammalian brains are pretty peaceful fellows, and what's more, they aren't your friends in one generation and your enemies in the next.

Rears Its Ugly Head

Sex is another good example of how the political cortex has botched things up. It couldn't possibly look you in the eye and say with a straight face that it wouldn't like to give in (openly, not just undercover) to every lovely lust of its neighbor downstairs—even as it passes laws against abortion, adultery, pornography, and holds itself above it all.

On the other hand, the old instinctual brain plays no phony games nor denies all sorts of juicy appetites and proclivities, libidinous and otherwise. Why not have a little fun getting the job done? Everything's out in the open and neither a rat nor a rhinoceros is ashamed of it.

But the political brain, like the reformed prostitute, has so bad-mouthed the libertine life it loves so well that it's even given sex, the mother and father of us all, a bad name. However, it's only because of the company it kept. It got sucked in against its inclinations by its first cousin, the religious cortex, encased in the fragile skulls of prophets like Mohammed, Moses, and Jesus. They sold the gullible political cortex a bill of goods in an all-out war against sin and corruption, and he was boxed in. How in the world could a politician, the cortex of all people, not go against corruption? But then, who'd have thought that that pious believer brain would have double-crossed him and slipped sex into the sin category?

The Inquisition was the finest hour of the alliance of the political and religious brains against their instinctual half. And this unholy alliance is not dead, no matter how much the political brain pontificates on the separation of church and state. This deal has not only managed to take much of the fun out of life, but it has also caused more misery than sin could possibly have in five hundred years of the wildest orgies.

To top this off (mucking up sex and territory), the callow new cortex, typical of sniveling youth, points its finger and blames corruption yet on his poor old grandaddy, whining "he did it" as soon as he's caught. Born with less than a saintly inheritance, the new brain knows in its heart that corruption was a human invention. In the Federalist papers, our Founding Fathers admit that all men are corrupt—and for every new brainey corruptee there is a corrupter. But even if by chance corruption didn't come with birth, a politician's own Ontogeny in the smoke-filled womb could pervert even the most innocent political talent. The angel Gabriel could never have withstood the ravages of the club, the campaign, or the convention.

There is not a scintilla of proof that even the scurviest of instinctual brains—even the sneaky hyena leader—ever demanded a kickback or a rakeoff, nor has one baboon chief ever been indicted by any jury of its peers for malfeasance in office. Has any beast below *Homo politicus* ever been known to have conceived anything resembling the Agnew "envelopes," the ITT arrangement, or the milk coops' "exchange"?

Animal is Beautiful

Though the fresh new cortex has muscle and uses it, the old one doesn't roll over and play dead. The old political workhorse in the lower cranial reaches is no pushover—not by a long shot. These elder statesmen aren't flashy, have built no monuments to themselves, written no political tomes, fabricated no great treaties, created no détentes, jacked up no interest rates, and pulled no wheat deals like the cortex, but they have a way of life that works. And what's more, they've been consistent for billions of years. The steady lower brain has its eye on one goal only—survival (something the political cortex handles much too casually). It can't be condemned for that.

However, the lower brains are neither all that perfect—nor successful. Occasionally, the old instinct will show its crocodile temper or its nasty puff adder sensitivity—but only when provoked. (Strangely enough, the cortex, if it communicates at all with instincts, it's only with the dregs like the two mentioned.)

Though these elder statesmen have lost a few too, like the mammoth and the ichthyosauros, they've won a million others from the slug to the orangutan, all on their own, which is saying a lot. The new cortex, spanning only these few million years from the oldest australopithecine to the present, has only one contest under its belt—*man*, a big one to be sure, but only one.

We can't be too ungrateful. The political cortex hasn't done too badly by us—or itself—in the past two million years. But what worries us is the next hundred. It's worrisome because the two brains seem poles apart, which poses some big problems for the preservation of us all (the bailiwick of the instinct). The arrogant way the cortex is going about things may just be too much for the lower brain's good sense to beat. Ordinarily, the cortex, the big boss, should show some *noblesse oblige*— even if only to save its own neck. But it doesn't, not a bit—it won't give in. In fact, just the reverse. When the lower cousin shivers at the thought of the cortex pulling tricks like the nuclear deterrent or brinksmanship, it gets nothing for its concern, only abuse and calumny (yet what did gunpowder deter?). It's even looked down on by the political cortex as if it were some sort of an undesirable saying "how could an animal brain understand this sort of sophisticated idea"? But sooner or later, if the political intellect doesn't do us all in, it must see the light that Animal is Beautiful—and could even be conducive to longevity.

Wither Trizophrenia?

So there he stands on the Capitol steps, outwardly calm, cool, a bit overbearing, but harboring a trizoid brain full of conflict and hiding an integration problem that'll take more than bussing or sit-ins to solve. And if he is going to be helped, it better be soon. For that new brain of his is coming up with the same old cliches of geopolitics, balance of power, treaties, and détentes that may be a great boon to the population problem, but plays havoc with the peace of mind.

At this stage of the game, with all of his supposed intellectual know-how, the politician is sitting on the fence with his finger in the air, his ears to the ground, and that combative trizoid brain still split three ways for Sunday. This is not very consoling, and what's more, there is no way to predict the outcome—neither his or ours.

However, there are a few straws in the wind that might give

us an inkling of things to come. Up until recently, democracy was the thing the new political mind was proudest of—ruling by, of, and for its very own cortex. What a triumph of man over jungle rule—*Liberté, Egalité, et Fraternité*. But only a few centuries after starting that idea, the same political brain completely reversed itself—and abandoning intellect, freedom, and the two-party system in favor of the master plan of that acortical genius of organization, the flying ant.

The Soviets were the first. Not only did they plagiarize the system from a termite without a single cortical cell behind its proboscis, but today, all of their followers—Cuba, China, etc.—even mimic the termite's old-fashioned caste system. They have look-alike hives to sleep in, look-alike borsch to drink, look-alike Mao jackets to wear, and think-alike slogans to live by. It appears that the new cortex voluntarily put itself in cold storage. So here we are in the latter part of the twentieth century and suddenly instinct is alive and well again, ruling the human termitarium as in the good old days.

The irony to end all ironies is that of all the political innovators, who but the godless, iconoclastic People's Republics would take the old biblical admonishment and heed it: "Go to the ant thou sluggard, consider her ways and be wise."

This back-tracking to the ways of the insect means either that the new political brain is getting soft in the head and is throwing in the sponge, or it's gripped by a temporary insanity like populism or the New Politics. We're not sure which.

The Brain Wane

Another clue, if a cloudy one, also seems to be telling us that the supersophisticated political cortex may be going the way of all other ordinary brains—down. We know that as the new brain gets bigger and more creative, it intimidates and weakens even the most useful and benign instincts. Einstein and Whitehead were so brainy they literally had to be told when to eat and practically led to the bathroom. In Great Britain (and elsewhere), Oxford graduates frequently take courses in intercourse (postgraduate)—they've forgotten how. If this becomes more prevalent and the cortex continues to grow, it will not only put the instinctual brain completely out of business, but it will also self-destruct. For if the last hundred years is any yardstick, as the political brain grew, the more lethal aspects of man's nature ran amok. Coupled with the sterility of the Oxford syndrome, it would only be a matter of time before it all goes down the drain.

Closer study (and the observation that the Nobel Committee has to scrape the barrel for recipients of its peace prizes) seem to show these intellectual giants—these brainy mutants —are not invading the political sphere. In fact, the trend is just the opposite. It appears that anthropoidal, raunchy, chomping, brawling Neanderthals are inheriting the earth. Though they could teach that Oxford *course called inter* without preparation, outline, or notes, these evolving new humans have to literally count on their fingers and toes to figure out a subway fare. And if, as the behaviorists say, from here on in man's evolution is in his culture, so *Gangbusters, Bonanza,* the new communes, pot, uppers, downers, Watkins Glen, and Woodstock will take us back to where we came from. But as Lorenz says, "It may be an improvement, the only beings on earth in which only the most intelligent govern are the monkeys and baboons; not by the strongest, but rather by the scientists and the sages because there is among them a veritable senate of experienced beings who make the decisions."

And though the saner brain falls mainly on the wane, it's not fast enough. We're caught betwixt and between, with specimens such as Lester Maddox, Sam Yorty, and Spiro Agnew. Only halfway back to baboondom, here we are in political limbo. This is not the first time this would have happened in biologic history. At about the time of man's emergence, the superintelligent dolphin, then a land animal, sensed the inevitable and he'd have none of it. It was back to the sea for him.

The Mind Leading the Mind

Whether the politician winds up following his cortex or his old instinct, it looks like he comes to no good. As Justice Thurgood Marshall used to open his speeches on black progress in America to African students, "Where is we now at?" It s hard to say. The only hope is that the other more successful brain types might bring their poor, dumb political cousin to his senses to make peace with his elders. But it's the mind leading the mind, and so far the best they have come up with is psychoanalysis and group encounters, which have helped mainly the psychiatrists' accounts receivable.

For instance the ordinary non-political follower brain which aids and abets the political process couldn't and wouldn't rise up and smite the ways of its master with the jawbone of an ass. Not likely when he sits on the same fence as his master.

The artistic brains have tried through their best and bravest such as Jane Fonda in Hanoi, Frank Sinatra and Sammy Davis, Jr., in the White House, and others like Casals and Picasso. The scientific intellect of physicist Edward Teller and Dr. Spock have taken a shot at it, only to make things more confusing.

Could the highly respected, overly touted, brain of the so-called *political* scientist heal itself? Could the social philosopher, and the behavioral expert get together long enough to help this brain integration? They'd be the least likely to succeed. First of all, they'd never sit down at the same lunch counter together. Secondly, most of them have already compounded the malfeasance of the trizophrenic brain with their plans and systems.

Genius do-gooders from Jesus to Mao have come up with plans such as the Essene Kingdom of Heaven, the Empire the sun never sets on, and now the impeccable apiarylike People's Republic. None have helped soothe the politician's savage cortex.

Who else? The facile brain of the press? We might have taken a flyer on them, but with their abysmal showing in Watergate, they'd probably drag their feet till it's too late. They're also too erratic and power-prone. In any event, they themselves are clinging to a cliff by their fingernails so they can't be bothered with worthy causes.

Well, when all else fails, we pray. But there is an old brain score to be settled here, too. When the first godly man came down from his first conference with his "maker," the chiseled tablets firmly in hand, it was a day of infamy. For from then on, the soul was set up as a preserve for the cortex only. No sinful animal brains were allowed, even with every Tom, Dick, and Harry on the human cannibal circuit. When it comes down to it, what with noncelebate priests and rock masses, the Father, the Son, and the Holy Ghost haven't yet solved their own problems.

Could lightning strike again, as it did in the alluvial slime when it created life, and bring these two brains together? Could some genius or miracle do it? Arthur Koestler, who has pondered this dilemma for a decade, comes up with the measly hope that a "harmonizing hormone will be discovered for resolving the intellectual and emotional conflict" (that was only in the ordinary brain—he didn't mention the political one).

And Dr. Paul McLean, who knows more about trizophrenia than any man alive, states that the "struggle reflects the established organization of man's brain," then practically throws up his hands as he concludes vapidly, "The best hope for salvation lies in education and enlightenment." What with—a political retardee?

The Browning of America

What is left—Consciousness III? If so, "All hope abandon ye who enter here." Can aspirin cure a splitting headache like trizophrenia? Even Consciousness VI or X could only portend a *browning* rather than a *greening* of America.

The cry has always been, "Let human nature do it." But there ain't no human nature here but us animals. Leaving it to the political Noble Savage's good offices is an exercise in glory—a path leading only to the same grave of the dodo and the pterodactyl, a bag of bones to be dug up and wired together for some nice Martian family to visit on a rainy Sunday afternoon in a hereafter museum. It may take a million years or happen tomorrow morning after breakfast. In any event, it seems that never the thrain shall meet.

> Ashes to Ashes and Bones to Bones
> If the cortex don't get us
> It's back to the clones

So with malice toward none and charity to all, pity the poor politician. Even as he and his genetic foibles led us to the White House, now downward and backward he points us to whence we came. It's been a good ride while it lasted. As a creature of his beginnings, we must forgive him, for he knows not what he does.